The
Ultimate Guide to
Astrology

USE THE GUIDANCE OF THE PLANETS TO
MANIFEST YOUR POWER AND PURPOSE

Tanaaz Chubb

FAIR WINDS

© 2021 Quarto Publishing Group USA Inc.
Text © 2021 Tanaaz Chubb

First Published in 2021 by Fair Winds Press, an imprint of The Quarto Group,
100 Cummings Center, Suite 265-D, Beverly, MA 01915, USA.
T (978) 282-9590 F (978) 283-2742 QuartoKnows.com

Fair Winds Press titles are also available at discount for retail, wholesale, promotional, and bulk purchase. For details, contact the Special Sales Manager by email at specialsales@quarto.com or by mail at The Quarto Group, Attn: Special Sales Manager, 100 Cummings Center, Suite 265-D, Beverly, MA 01915, USA.

25 24 23 22 21   1 2 3 4 5

ISBN: 978-1-58923-987-6

Digital edition published in 2021
eISBN: 978-1-58923-988-3

Library of Congress Cataloging-in-Publication Data

Names: Chubb, Tanaaz, author.
Title: The ultimate guide to astrology : use the guidance of the planets to
    manifest your power and purpose / Tanaaz Chubb.
Description: Beverly : Fair Winds Press, 2021. | Series: The ultimate guide
    to... | Includes index. | Summary: "With The Ultimate Guide to
    Astrology, leading astrologer and Instagram star Tanaaz Chubb presents a
    modern and accessible approach to astrology with an emphasis on the
    signs and the planets"-- Provided by publisher.
Identifiers: LCCN 2020052521 (print) | LCCN 2020052522 (ebook) | ISBN
    9781589239876 (trade paperback) | ISBN 9781589239883 (ebook)
Subjects: LCSH: Astrology. | Astrology and vocational guidance.
Classification: LCC BF1708.1 .C48 2021 (print) | LCC BF1708.1 (ebook) |
    DDC 133.5--dc23
LC record available at https://lccn.loc.gov/2020052521
LC ebook record available at https://lccn.loc.gov/2020052522

Design: Allison Meierding
Page Layout: Allison Meierding
Cover Illustration: Suzanne Washington
Illustration: Suzanne Washington with additional flourishes by Shutterstock

Printed in China

DEDICATION

Dedicated to my dear friend, Rachel,
who first introduced me to the magic of astrology.

CONTENTS

Introduction

Astrology is the study of our connection to the cosmos. "As above, so below" is the guiding principle: Whatever is happening in the sky above can give us clues as to what is happening within, and vice versa. At the moment when you were born, the planets and stars all aligned in a configuration that is unique to you. This configuration of planets holds the energetic blueprint of your soul and the energetic forces that surround you as you walk this journey.

I was first introduced to astrology by my friend Rachel. Prior to this, I thought astrology was reading your weekly horoscope. It wasn't until Rachel drew my birth chart—based on my date, place, and time of birth—that my interest in astrology started to grow. Even though Rachel knew a lot about me already, as she read my birth chart, there were things she was saying and dates she was giving me that seemed to align perfectly with experiences I had gone through. I was so taken by everything she shared that it kick-started my own journey with astrology.

Through the years, astrology has helped me peel back the layers to reveal new truths and insights about myself. It has allowed me to see what energies I am working with in this life and how I can use them as strengths. Astrology gently guides you to understand the different energetic frequencies that you can harness to lead a balanced, connected, and richer life. It can also highlight some lessons your soul has come to learn and why certain vibrations or themes may be present.

While the study of astrology is endless, this book will break down the basic components and set you on the path to reading and understanding the vibrations that surround you and what messages they hold for you. Get ready to connect with the cosmic skies, the cosmic blueprint of your soul, and the foundation of the ancient art of astrology. Enjoy the journey!

YOUR MAP TO THE COSMIC SKIES

Astrology is an ancient art that connects the Universe around you to the Universe within you. As you start your journey, you will see that there is a formula or chart system that is used to help make sense of the planets, the zodiac signs, and the energies they are creating. This chart system is like your map to the stars. Once you understand the basics of it, you will be able to read your own chart, the charts of others, and the chart of our present time as well.

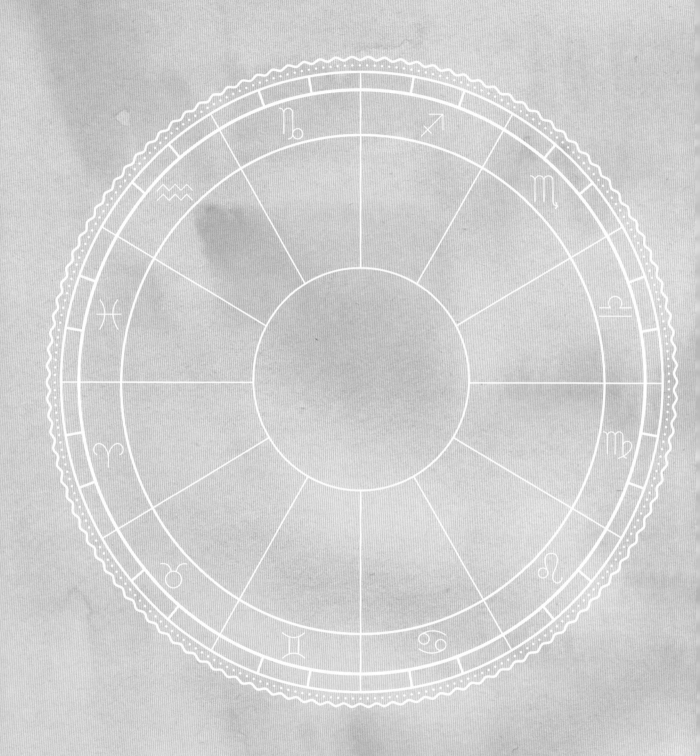

1

Your Birth Chart: Decoding the Cosmos Within

The best place to start when it comes to studying astrology is your own birth chart. This chapter explains the important components: the houses, sacred angles, and aspects. As you decode your chart, you'll begin to learn more about astrology and have a deeper understanding of yourself. Once you see your birth chart, you may wonder how you are ever going to understand it all! Don't worry, I am here to guide you, and I promise it is a lot easier than it looks.

HOUSES

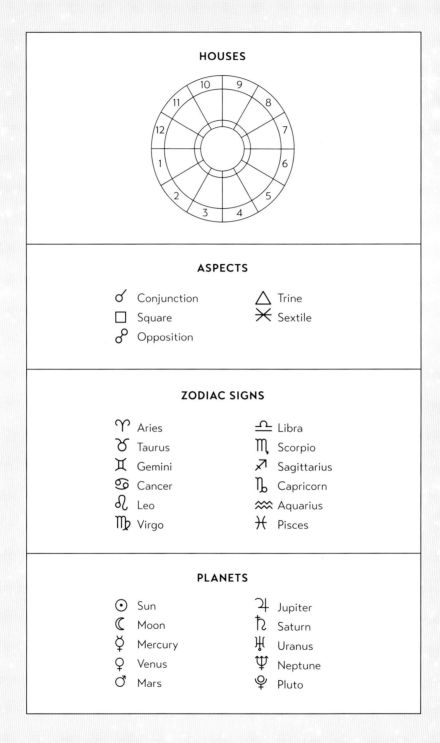

ASPECTS

☌ Conjunction	△ Trine
☐ Square	✳ Sextile
☍ Opposition	

ZODIAC SIGNS

♈ Aries	♎ Libra
♉ Taurus	♏ Scorpio
♊ Gemini	♐ Sagittarius
♋ Cancer	♑ Capricorn
♌ Leo	♒ Aquarius
♍ Virgo	♓ Pisces

PLANETS

☉ Sun	♃ Jupiter
☾ Moon	♄ Saturn
☿ Mercury	♅ Uranus
♀ Venus	♆ Neptune
♂ Mars	♇ Pluto

DRAWING AND DECODING YOUR CHART

For the most accurate birth chart, you will need to know your exact time of birth. There are many free online tools that will draw your birth chart for you. For the purposes of this book, I recommend printing a copy of your chart and having it in front of you so it's easier to follow along.

If you don't know your birth time, draw your chart with the time set to 12 p.m. With this method, the house placements will not be accurate, so you won't be able to determine your rising sign (page 16) or other sacred angles (page 16). Nevertheless, you will still be able to build a great snapshot of the energies you are working with in this life.

When it comes to understanding your birth chart, there are four things to master:

Zodiac Signs

Houses and Sacred Angles

Planets

Aspects

HOUSES

In Western astrology, your chart is drawn as a wheel of 360 degrees. This wheel is divided into twelve sections or houses. Each house represents a different area of your life and your soul journey.

Each house is associated with one of the twelve zodiac signs. We'll learn more about that on page 23. When you look at your chart, you will notice that you have your own astrological signs for each house, making your chart unique! You will also see the planets sprinkled through your chart based on where they were at the time of your birth.

Because each house carries a particular theme, the zodiac sign and any planets within that house can indicate where you are likely to see the energy manifesting the most in your life. For example, the tenth house rules over your career, so any planet in this part of the chart is likely to express itself in your work or public life.

THE THEMES OF EACH HOUSE

FIRST HOUSE: **I AM**	*Natural rulers are Aries and the planet Mars*	Self, ego, your identity, your personality, your body, general temperament, early childhood, approach to life, physical health, vitality
SECOND HOUSE: **I POSSESS**	*Natural rulers are Taurus and the planet Venus*	Earned income, self-worth, material possessions, values, sense of security, confidence
THIRD HOUSE: **I EXPRESS**	*Natural rulers are Gemini and the planet Mercury*	Self-expression, mind, intellect, speaking, communication, siblings/cousins, domestic travel, coworkers, local neighborhood, perception of childhood, adaptability
FOURTH HOUSE: **I BELONG**	*Natural rulers are Cancer and the Moon*	Home and family life, property, who you are when no one is watching, real estate, domestic life, parents, later life, ancestry, private life, endings
FIFTH HOUSE: **I CREATE**	*Natural rulers are Leo and the Sun*	Creativity, children, romance, fun, pleasure, dating, artistic abilities, hobbies, recreational activities, gambling, pregnancy
SIXTH HOUSE: **I HEAL**	*Natural rulers are Virgo and the planet Mercury*	General health, productivity, your day-to-day routine, animals, duties, diet, fitness, energy level, workplace environment
SEVENTH HOUSE: **I CONNECT**	*Natural rulers are Libra and the planet Venus*	Relationships, how you relate to others, people you are in business with, contracts, contractual relationships, marriage, divorce, conflicts
EIGHTH HOUSE: **I TRANSFORM**	*Natural rulers are Scorpio and the planet Pluto*	Transformation, investments, inheritance, taxes, insurance, death and rebirth, the taboo, sex, drugs/alcohol, psychic, occult, sleep, surgery, joint finances, investigation, research
NINTH HOUSE: **I SEEK**	*Natural rulers are Sagittarius and the planet Jupiter*	Learning, teaching, higher education, higher mind, philosophy, publishing, justice, legal issues, international travel, humanitarian efforts, grandchildren, in-laws, law, ethics
TENTH HOUSE: **I PURSUE**	*Natural rulers are Capricorn and the planet Saturn*	Career, fame, public persona, purpose, reputation, status, ambitions, employer, government, desire for power, success, professional life
ELEVENTH HOUSE: **I DREAM**	*Natural rulers are Aquarius and the planet Uranus*	Friendships, community, groups or clubs, religion, hopes, dreams and wishes, technology, humanitarianism, group thinking, large social events, networking
TWELFTH HOUSE: **I TRANSCEND**	*Natural rulers are Pisces and the planet Neptune*	Secrets, struggles, the unconscious, behind-the-scenes, shadow self, psychic gifts, karma, jails, hospitals, subconscious mind, intuition, healing, confinement, self-sabotage, escapism

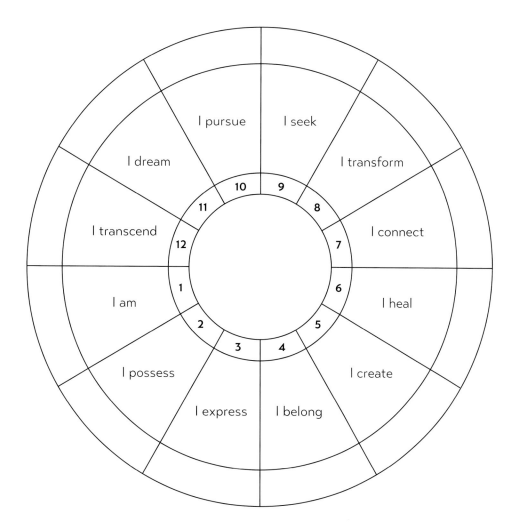

EMPTY HOUSES

· · · · · · · · · ·

If a house is empty, check which zodiac sign rules over that house in your own chart to see what qualities would be most active in that part of your life. For example, if Gemini is the ruler of your tenth house, when it comes to your career, you may find yourself tapping into the gift of communication that Gemini can bring.

SACRED ANGLES

The twelve houses of your chart are all important; however, there are four angles that carry extra significance. These four angles are ruled by a different sign of the zodiac, and they will be unique to you. You need to know your time of birth to accurately understand your sacred angles.

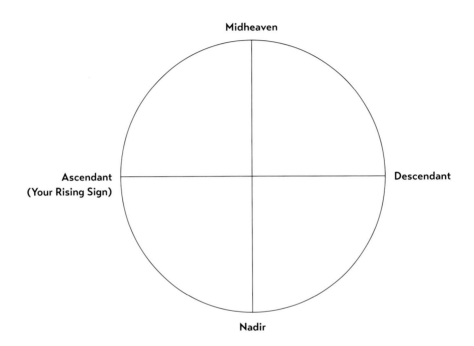

The Ascendant or Rising Sign

The ascendant or rising sign is located between the twelfth and first house. It is the zodiac that was on the horizon at the time of your birth. Think of your rising sign as the starting point to your entire chart. It is the doorway that paves the way to everything else, and it is as important as your Sun sign (page 38). Your rising sign represents the "outer" you, the person you are before someone gets to know you.

DON'T KNOW YOUR BIRTH TIME?

If you don't know your time of birth, determining your rising sign can be done intuitively or with an astrologer. If you want to use the intuitive method, simply read the interpretations (page 17) and see which one stands out the most to you.

YOUR RISING SIGN

Aries Rising	*Ruled by Mars*	You appear as confident, courageous, and bold. You are a go-getter, very headstrong, and you love to do things your own way. Be mindful of overcommitting yourself or agreeing to more than you can handle. It's okay to release control and ask for help when you need it.
Taurus Rising	*Ruled by Venus*	You are down-to-earth and easygoing, but there is a lot going on beneath the surface that many wouldn't be privy to. You are loyal and responsible, and people tend to trust you easily.
Gemini Rising	*Ruled by Mercury*	You are friendly, sociable, and seem to get along well with everyone. You are good at adapting to whatever situation you find yourself in. Make sure you aren't sacrificing too much of yourself to fit in.
Cancer Rising	*Ruled by the Moon*	You are sensitive and caring but also fiercely loyal and protective. When you care about something, you will do all you can to defend and look after it. You have a strong intuition, too, so be sure to listen to its wisdom.
Leo Rising	*Ruled by the Sun*	You have a fun-loving energy, and you tend to thrive when you are in the spotlight and when you feel passionate about something. You are vibrant and warm, and have a creative spark that shines through your eyes.
Virgo Rising	*Ruled by Mercury*	You are practical, well organized, and you know how to keep your composure no matter what is happening around you. You are a natural caregiver and are compassionate and considerate of others. Make sure you are treating yourself with the same loving-kindness that you so easily show to others.
Libra Rising	*Ruled by Venus*	You have a way of making everyone around you feel comfortable. You seem to know what others need and are in tune with your environment and surroundings. Your keen insights make you a great people person, and you have a way of easily soothing tensions and finding the middle ground. Make sure you are not losing sight of yourself in your efforts to help and support others.
Scorpio Rising	*Ruled by Pluto*	You have a way of drawing people in with your highly magnetic and attractive energy. You may come across as secretive or a little mysterious, and this is because you have many complex layers that make up who you are. You and those you let in will never be bored, for you are always traveling deeper and looking to understand yourself from new depths.

table continues

Sagittarius Rising	*Ruled by Jupiter*	You have a way of lighting up whatever room you walk into. People are drawn to your sunny personality and your playful and carefree attitude. You have the gift of seeing the lighter side of life, and by embracing this, you can remain cool, calm, and collected in the midst of chaos. You are always searching for adventure, just don't forget to balance your responsibilities as well.
Capricorn Rising	*Ruled by Saturn*	On the surface you can appear a little serious and maybe even closed off, but as soon as people get to know you, your witty sense of humor, intelligence, and warm personality can shine through. You are hardworking, responsible, and highly motivated and ambitious when you put your mind to something.
Aquarius Rising	*Ruled by Uranus*	You beat to the tune of your own drum and do things in your own way. You love sharing your wisdom, resources, and ideas, and you are always willing to lend a hand. While you are social and friendly to all, you are also a private person, and it can take a while before you feel comfortable opening up and expressing your true self.
Pisces Rising	*Ruled by Neptune*	You are a gentle, imaginative soul who likes to daydream and fantasize. You can use your imagination to create whole new worlds and bring them to life using your creativity. You can get lost in your mind at times, so make sure you are grounding yourself in the present moment.

The Descendant

The descendant sits between your sixth and seventh houses. The sign here indicates how you relate to and connect with others. It also indicates one of the signs that you may be most compatible with.

The Midheaven

The midheaven sits between your ninth and tenth houses. The sign here indicates how you approach your career and passions and how you go after fulfilling your purpose. The sign that rules over your midheaven is also the energy or quality that can connect you with your higher self or to the power of your soul.

The Nadir

The nadir is located on the cusp between the third and the fourth houses. It indicates your inner needs and unconscious behaviors that you need to become aware of to understand who you are on the deepest of levels. The nadir is a highly spiritually charged point on the chart that indicates the energy or quality you need to tap into to become more authentic. Being true to yourself is a valuable spiritual mission. The zodiac ruler of the nadir can give you clues on how to go about this. Read the description of the zodiac sign of your nadir and see if you can be open to this energy.

ASPECTS

Another key piece to decoding and understanding your chart is the aspects. Aspects are the way in which the planets in your chart communicate and connect with each other. Depending on the astrological software used to draw your chart, you should notice the aspects as lines crisscrossing in the center of your chart. When certain planets align with each other, they can take on extra significance and carry a more pronounced energy.

Aspects can be challenging to understand, especially when you are first starting. Don't worry about grasping it straight away.

THE MAJOR ASPECTS

Aspect	Symbol	Degrees	Meaning
Conjunction	☌	0	Indicates their energy merging as one and becoming stronger
Square	☐	90	Indicates tension, but this tension also helps create action
Opposition	☍	180	Indicates balance that needs to be found between the two planets
Trine	△	120	Indicates harmony, protection, and luck
Sextile	⚹	60	Indicates ease, simplicity, and harmony

As understanding aspects is advanced, we will not be exploring them further in this book. If you feel ready, make a list of all the squares, trines, sextiles, and so on in your chart and use the planetary descriptions that follow to see how they may interact with one another.

ORBS

Orbs are the "grace" degrees given for each of the aspects. While a square is classically represented by two planets being 90 degrees apart, a margin of 5 to 10 degrees can be given. These margins are called orbs. Orbs vary depending on the preference of the astrologer.

BRINGING IT ALL TOGETHER

Astrology can sometimes feel overwhelming, but remember that it's an intuitive art. Now that you have the foundation of your astrology chart and you understand its basic components, we will dive deeper into the meaning of each zodiac sign, the planets, and what they mean in the corresponding houses. This is where we can see it all come together!

DRAW YOUR OWN BIRTH CHART

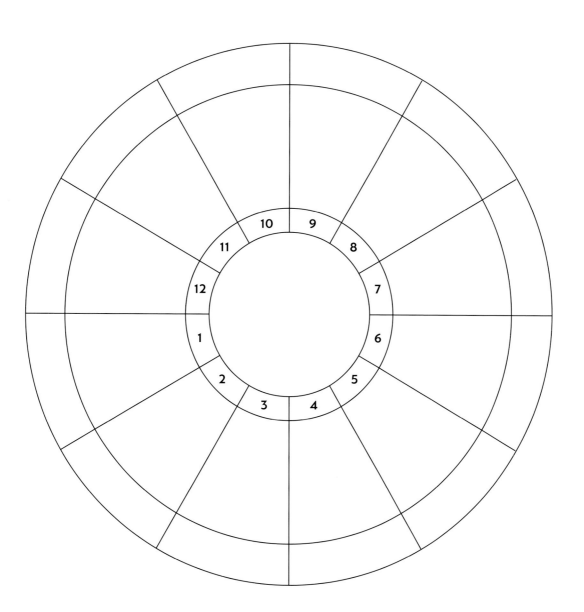

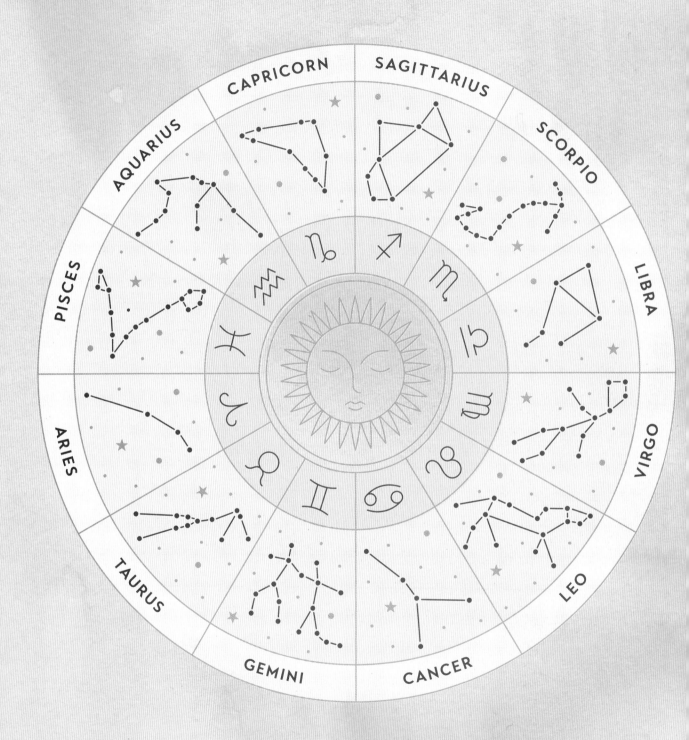

CHAPTER

Zodiac Signs

In traditional Western astrology, we use twelve zodiac signs. As you will see as you work through this book, we each have the twelve energies of the zodiac somewhere in our chart. What you read here is the essence of these zodiac energies that are alive and present in each and every one of us regardless of what our Sun sign may be. We can tap into these energies through our planets, at the corresponding time of year, or when we are in need of that particular energy in our lives.

♈ ARIES   ♉ TAURUS   ♊ GEMINI

♋ CANCER   ♌ LEO   ♍ VIRGO

♎ LIBRA   ♏ SCORPIO   ♐ SAGITTARIUS

♑ CAPRICORN   ♒ AQUARIUS   ♓ PISCES

ZODIAC SIGNS: ELEMENTS & QUALITIES

The twelve zodiac signs are each assigned an element and a quality. The elements are earth, air, fire, and water. The qualities are cardinal, mutable, and fixed. Think of the qualities like the changing seasons from summer to autumn and winter to spring. The zodiac signs that begin a season are cardinal, the signs at the middle of the season are fixed, and the signs at the end of the season just before they change are mutable.

Elements
- Earth: grounded, stable, solid
- Air: inspired, thoughtful, imaginative
- Fire: passionate, impulsive, energetic
- Water: sensitive, emotional, fluid

Qualities
- Cardinal Signs: leader, starter, headstrong
- Fixed Signs: stubborn, focused, persistent
- Mutable Signs: adaptable, accommodating, flexible

ZODIAC SIGNS: ELEMENTS & QUALITIES

Zodiac	Element	Quality
Aries	Fire	Cardinal
Taurus	Earth	Fixed
Gemini	Air	Mutable
Cancer	Water	Cardinal
Leo	Fire	Fixed
Virgo	Earth	Mutable
Libra	Air	Cardinal
Scorpio	Water	Fixed
Sagittarius	Fire	Mutable
Capricorn	Earth	Cardinal
Aquarius	Air	Fixed
Pisces	Water	Mutable

ENERGETIC EXPRESSIONS

Let's now look at the energetic expression of each zodiac sign.

Aries

DATES March 21–April 19

SYMBOL Ram

ELEMENT Fire

QUALITY Cardinal

RULING PLANET Mars

BODY PARTS head, face, eyes

AFFIRMATION I am Energy

KEYWORDS leader, starter, creative, aggressive, innovative

Aries is the first sign of the zodiac. Its energy is synonymous with new beginnings and leadership. Aries is the birthplace of all creation—the seed before it's planted. Who knows what it may grow to become, but that seed holds so much potential and creative energy just waiting to unfold. Aries is full of life, fiery and expressive, and ready to lead the way.

Aries is represented by the horns of the headstrong ram due to its independence and the fact that it likes to be in charge. Aries is passionate, impatient, impulsive, and, at times, aggressive. We can tune in to Aries energy, the birthplace of creation, whenever we are looking to manifest, create, or gain some confidence in getting a project off the ground. Aries energy is naturally invigorating and energizing, and it reminds us that all of creation first started as energy.

Taurus

DATES April 20–May 20

SYMBOL Bull

ELEMENT Earth

QUALITY Fixed

RULING PLANET Venus

BODY PARTS throat, neck, ears, vocal cords

AFFIRMATION I am Abundant

KEYWORDS reliable, consistent, abundant, pleasure seeking, sluggish

Taurus is the second sign of the zodiac. Its energetic quality is like nature in full bloom. It's abundant, sensual, and associated with desire and pleasure. Its energy is slow moving, but it has power to go the distance. It likes to build step by step and brick by brick in a structured and orderly way. Taurus can be sluggish when it comes to change.

It is represented by the bull because of its strength but also stubbornness and sometimes rigid behavior. We can call on Taurus energy when we need to feel grounded, to welcome abundance and a greater sense of self-worth into our lives, and to summon the stamina to go the distance.

Gemini

DATES May 21–June 20
SYMBOL Twins
ELEMENT Air
QUALITY Mutable
RULING PLANET Mercury

BODY PARTS arms, hands, lungs, nervous system
AFFIRMATION I am Expressive
KEYWORDS intellectual, quick-witted, communicator, messenger

Gemini is the third sign of the zodiac. Its essence is about mind, body, and spirit coming together as one. When we are in this state of alignment, we can be ourselves and express whatever is on our mind and in our heart. Gemini is intellectual, social, and adaptable to its environment. We can call on Gemini energy whenever we need confidence and charisma in social settings or when we are looking to communicate our thoughts and feelings.

Gemini is represented by the twins. One twin is mortal, the other is immortal or not of this world, signifying the balance between working through life on a physical, human level and also on an energetic, soul level. It is Gemini that forms a bridge between these two realms, allowing us to operate as both human and *being*.

Cancer

DATES June 21–July 22
SYMBOL Crab
ELEMENT Water
QUALITY Cardinal
RULING PLANET Moon

BODY PARTS chest, breasts, stomach
AFFIRMATION I am Love
KEYWORDS sensitive, intuitive, nurturing, compassionate, moody

Cancer is the fourth sign of the zodiac. It encourages us to open our hearts, to love ourselves, and to work on feeling at peace within ourselves. Cancer can highlight our emotional state, but it also encourages us to accept ourselves, forgive, and move through the world with compassion.

In the Greek myth of the Cancer constellation, the crab was a fearless and compassionate protector of all sea life. One day, it risked its life to warn another sea creature that was in danger. A goddess witnessed the crab's bravery, so she threw its broken pieces into the sky, forming the constellation of the crab to remind us of the importance of standing up for ourselves and others in times of need or injustice. We can tune in to Cancer energy whenever we need compassion and nourishment, but also when we are looking for strength to stand up for those we love and for what we believe in.

Leo

DATES July 23–August 22

SYMBOL Lion

ELEMENT Fire

QUALITY Fixed

RULING PLANET Sun

BODY PARTS heart, spine, gallbladder

AFFIRMATION I am Strong

KEYWORDS fiery, bold, fun-loving, playful, creative, proud

Leo is the fifth sign of the zodiac. It is a highly creative, confident, and fun-loving energy. The essence of Leo is light, and its energy guides us to stand tall and shine our light for the whole world to see.

Represented by the lion, Leo has energy we can call on whenever we need a boost of confidence, to feel strong and secure in ourselves and when we want to share our creative gifts and talents with the world. Leo is generous: it moves quickly and activates feelings of strength and pride but also fun and laughter. It is highly magnetic and allows us to draw and manifest things into our reality with ease.

Virgo

DATES August 23–September 22

SYMBOL Virgin

ELEMENT Earth

QUALITY Mutable

RULING PLANET Mercury

BODY PARTS digestive system, intestines, pancreas

AFFIRMATION I am Whole

KEYWORDS perfectionist, independent, healing, self-sufficient

Virgo is the sixth sign of the zodiac. It is represented by the virgin—but this word has taken on a new meaning since this sign was named. The virgin is about independence. It is about finding strength and fulfillment from within, without needing another person for validation. Virgo is analytical, practical, and precise.

We can call on Virgo energy when we need support with analytical thinking or when we need to get organized. It's also a strong energy to call on for healing. Virgo allows us to remember the inner strength and intuition that we possess and can use to guide us through all sorts of challenges, particularly around our health and well-being.

Libra

DATES September 23–October 22

SYMBOL Scales

ELEMENT Air

QUALITY Cardinal

RULING PLANET Venus

BODY PARTS kidneys, appendix, skin

AFFIRMATION I am Balanced

KEYWORDS relationships, peace, balance, fairness, harmony

Libra is the seventh sign of the zodiac. It is keeper of the scales and carries the energy of justice, harmony, and peace. Libra allows us to see both sides of the coin and to weigh our options. As the sign of justice, it allows us to fight for what we believe in.

Libra guides us to step out of our own inner world and put ourselves in the shoes of others. By seeing the world in this way, Libra lets us develop more thoughtful and fulfilling relationships. We can call on Libra energy to help us through disagreements, to guide us to see the other person's perspective, and when we need support to balance our emotions or to give and receive energy in our lives. Although Libra is an air sign, its energy guides us to stay balanced no matter what is happening around us.

Scorpio

DATES October 23–November 21

SYMBOL Scorpion

ELEMENT Water

QUALITY Fixed

RULING PLANET Pluto

BODY PARTS sex organs, reproductive system, colon, bladder

AFFIRMATION I am Transforming

KEYWORDS rebirth, renewal, intense, intuitive, obsessive

Scorpio is the eighth sign of the zodiac. It is highly transformative and guides us to keep digging deeper to turn our wounds into light. When Scorpio energy is free to go with the flow, transformation can happen easily and effortlessly; when the energy is resisted, tension and intensity can be created. Whenever you are going through a significant period of change or upheaval, call on Scorpio energy to help you navigate through this period of transformation and remind yourself that endings always lead to new beginnings.

Scorpio is ruled by the scorpion, a small yet powerful creature that, like a snake, has the power to shed its own skin to rebirth itself. Ultimately, Scorpio allows us to release what is no longer working in order to rebirth it into something new.

Sagittarius

DATES November 22–December 21

SYMBOL Arrow of the Archer

ELEMENT Fire

QUALITY Mutable

RULING PLANET Jupiter

BODY PARTS hips, sciatic nerve, liver

AFFIRMATION I am Wisdom

KEYWORDS expansive, optimistic, adventurous, scattered, visionary

Sagittarius is the ninth sign of the zodiac. It is represented by the arrow of the archer. While the archer is responsible for shooting the arrow, it is the arrow that gets to take flight, soar through the air, and make its target. The essence of Sagittarius is freedom—the ability to take aim and land where it needs to.

Sagittarius is an optimistic, adventurous, and bountiful energy that we can all call on when we are looking for more freedom, play, and excitement in our lives. It is also deeply philosophical and allows us to tap into the inner wisdom that we possess. Sagittarius reminds us that we always know the way forward and that we have all we need inside of us, we just have to give ourselves the right guidance and nurturing to release the pearls of wisdom that are hidden within.

Capricorn

DATES December 22–January 19

SYMBOL Sea Goat

ELEMENT Earth

QUALITY Cardinal

RULING PLANET Saturn

BODY PARTS knees, skeletal system, teeth

AFFIRMATION I am Responsible

KEYWORDS ambitious, disciplined, practical, deep, masterful

Capricorn is the tenth sign of the zodiac. It is represented by the sea goat, which is a mythical creature that is half fish, half goat. Its watery, fish quality means that it has the ability to swim in the depths of the ocean, but its goat body means that it also understands what it is like to walk on the earth. This combination of awareness makes Capricorn highly disciplined and wise. We can call on Capricorn energy when we are looking to find more ambition and when we need more motivation to get through life's challenges.

Capricorn is earthy, practical, and grounded, but this watery quality allows it to be intuitive too. By balancing the lessons of the deep, dark ocean, where it has to go with the flow, and the lessons of what it's like to be grounded on earth, Capricorn allows us to become masters of whatever challenges we are facing.

Aquarius

DATES January 20–February 18

SYMBOL Water Bearer

ELEMENT Air

QUALITY Fixed

RULING PLANET Uranus

BODY PARTS circulatory system, veins, ankles, calves

AFFIRMATION I am Connected

KEYWORDS humanitarian, progressive, original, rebellious, detached

Aquarius is the eleventh sign of the zodiac. Although it is an air sign, it is represented by the water bearer, who collects the heavy emotions of the planet in its vessel, then transforms and shifts them to higher levels of consciousness. Once this alchemy has taken place, the water bearer pours them back to Earth for people to drink.

Aquarius energy is healing. It guides us to remember that we are all connected and that when we work together, anything is possible. Its focus is on what is best for the greater good, rather than the individual. Its energy can create revolutions or inspire new ways of looking at things. We can call on Aquarius energy when we are looking for community, when we want to see things differently, and when we need to shift to higher consciousness.

Pisces

DATES February 19–March 20

SYMBOL Two Fish Swimming in Opposite Directions

ELEMENT Water

QUALITY Mutable

RULING PLANET Neptune

BODY PARTS feet, lymphatic system, immune system

AFFIRMATION I am Intuitive

KEYWORDS receptive, musical, sensitive, timid, spiritual

Pisces is the twelfth sign of the zodiac. It is represented by two fish swimming in opposite directions. As the last sign of the zodiac, Pisces is about completion and bringing an end to a chapter of our life journey. Whenever something comes to an end in our life, we can call on Pisces energy to guide us and to remind us that nothing is ever really lost. Just like energy cannot be destroyed, Pisces reminds us that all endings eventually pave the way to new beginnings.

The two fish swimming in opposite directions represent the yin and yang of life, but also the oneness that we are. Pisces is spiritual and helps us reconnect with the source that we all came from and will all return to. It reminds us that we are never alone on this journey and that we are here as part of a larger unfolding.

ZODIAC CHALLENGE

· · · · · · · · ·

Now that you have read through the description for each sign, see if you can fill in the following table, but try not to look back over the descriptions. See what you can remember—you may surprise yourself! The first one has been done for you.

Sign	Quality	Element	Symbol
Aries	Cardinal	Fire	Ram
Taurus			
Gemini			
Cancer			
Leo			
Virgo			
Libra			
Scorpio			
Sagittarius			
Capricorn			
Aquarius			
Pisces			

THE BLUEPRINT OF YOUR SOUL

While your entire chart tells your story, there are a few key components that paint a clear picture of some of the messages, lessons, and adventures that your soul set out to accomplish in this lifetime. These are your Sun sign, Moon sign, rising sign, and lunar nodes. As we have already looked at your rising sign, in this section, you will be taken on a journey to understand your Sun sign, Moon sign, and lunar nodes and how you can use these energies. Read for both the sign and the house, then blend the interpretations.

CHAPTER

3

The Sun

ZODIAC RULER Leo
KEYWORDS inner light, core self, ego
RULES OVER leadership, power, energy,
royalty, physicality, vitality

The Sun is the center of our solar system. Although it is located millions of miles away in our Milky Way galaxy, its rays are responsible for breathing life into every living thing on this planet. Understanding your Sun sign can give you clues into your essence. Your Sun sign represents what fuels you, what brings you vitality, and where you feel aligned. By acknowledging the energy behind your Sun sign, you can connect to your purpose and understand what you need to move through this world in a way that honors who you truly are.

☉ THE MEANING OF YOUR SUN SIGN

The Sun represents our life force energy and the core of who we are. It is the foundation of our personality and the key to feeling comfortable and at peace within ourselves. The Sun is dependable. It rises and sets every day, teaching us that there is always a new beginning on the horizon when things go dark. This same dependability and consistency can be found when we connect with our own center. From our center we find our strength, we find our peace, and we find the motivation to fulfill our destiny.

The astrological symbol for the Sun is a circle with a dot in the center. The outer circle represents the world around us, but that dot in the center is the true and constant us. It is our nature, our essence, the core or foundation of our being that is never wavering. Things may come and go from our life, things may feel chaotic around us, but like the Sun rising and setting each day, our core, our essence, is also unwavering.

To connect with the essence of your center and discover what will keep you feeling whole, take the journey into understanding your Sun sign.

☉♈ | SUN IN ARIES OR FIRST HOUSE

RULING PLANET Mars

KEYWORDS independent, entrepreneurial, energetic, leader

MOTIVATION to develop a strong sense of self

CHALLENGES temper, self-centered, impatient

AFFIRMATION I connect with my authentic self

No matter what hardships come your way, when you tune in to that inner Aries fire, you will find the strength, willpower, and determination to make it through to the other side. You shine when you are able to be independent and do things your way. You like to be in control, and while there may be times when this is necessary, you have to be mindful of becoming overly controlling or dominating the energy of others.

Learning to collaborate with others and release control is a valuable lesson when your Sun is in Aries. You are a strong leader and have an entrepreneurial spirit. You are gifted at coming up with new ideas, but may struggle to find the patience to see them through. This is where learning to collaborate and reach out for support can help you go that extra mile.

When not in balance, you can be quick to anger or may find yourself feeling fired up. Learning to process your emotions in a healthy way—and working from spirit rather than ego—will support you staying in alignment. You have a lot of headstrong energy that gives you this wonderful can-do attitude, but learning to shift energy from your mind to your heart will strengthen your intuition and allow you to feel more guided as you move through your journey.

The Sun entering Aries brings the start of the astrological year and the equinox. This is a time for new beginnings and to honor the cycle of death and rebirth. In the Northern Hemisphere, we can see new life in bloom. In the Southern Hemisphere, the leaves are falling as Mother Nature prepares to rest and retreat.

☉♉ | SUN IN TAURUS OR SECOND HOUSE

RULING PLANET Venus

KEYWORDS reliable, grounded, patient, creative

MOTIVATION to find true self-worth

CHALLENGES slow, stubborn, overindulgent

AFFIRMATION I am worthy just the way I am

You are grounded, methodical, and practical. This grounded energy comes from your desire to feel secure and stable as you move through your life journey. Deep in your subconscious, feeling safe is a driving motivation. There is nothing wrong with seeking comfort and safety, but you may find yourself stuck if you don't take the leap of faith and make changes as and when they are needed. You love things to be constant and crave routine—but learning to embrace change and go with the flow is a valuable lesson to keep in mind.

True safety is cultivated from within, so be mindful of looking to external sources to fulfill that desire in your life. Part of your journey in this life is learning to feel grounded in your inner power but be adaptable enough to surrender to the flow. Surrendering is not being passive: it's making choices and decisions from a place of trust and listening to the divine intelligence that flows freely within you.

You have the stamina and the patience to move through challenging projects and life events, and it is these qualities that become the mark of your success. When others give up or find the climb too difficult, you are there, still soldiering forward, using your slow and steady approach to win the race.

Lessons of self-worth are important for you. It can be tempting to measure your self-worth in the number of accolades you have or in how much money you make, but know that these measures are never going to fulfill you. When you can say "I am worthy" without any exceptions, you will feel more aligned and connected to your true essence.

You are a master builder and are here to take the seeds that have been planted and nurture them until they turn into forests. As the sign of Taurus is also connected to Mother Earth, you may feel soothed when surrounded by nature.

☉♊ | SUN IN GEMINI OR THIRD HOUSE

RULING PLANET Mercury

KEYWORDS versatile, communicative, social, curious

MOTIVATION to share wisdom and knowledge

CHALLENGES two-faced, manipulative, superficial

AFFIRMATION I attract positive thoughts into my life

You are a keen observer and are always interested in what others are thinking and feeling. Your mind is like a sponge, absorbing information from the world. You are quick-witted, and perhaps you always know the right things to say. Because your mind is like a computer picking up information, it is important that you learn how to filter what comes through. When you don't have a filter, your mind can become overwhelmed and you become prone to overthinking, anxiety, or stress. Having an outlet such as journaling or talking things through can also help.

You are a storyteller and can easily put yourself in another's shoes to convey emotion and help carry through a point. This incredible ability can be tempting to use to manipulate others to get your way, so be mindful of when you find yourself doing this.

As a Gemini Sun, your lesson in this life is to learn how to relax your mind and shift energy into your body. You can be so good at talking and taking in information that you can sometimes forget to actually experience life firsthand. It's one thing to read or think about life, but it's another thing to *live* it, and that's something to keep in mind.

Don't be afraid to live life wholeheartedly. Don't be afraid to step out of the clutches of your mind and get into your body. Take a moment to feel the aliveness of your body right now. When you align that aliveness with your sharp mind, that is when you can really thrive. You are a storyteller at heart, but the most powerful story you can tell is the one that you have walked yourself.

☉♋ | SUN IN CANCER OR FOURTH HOUSE

RULING PLANET Moon

KEYWORDS nurturing, emotional, intuitive, protective

MOTIVATION to find a sense of belonging

CHALLENGES defensive, possessive, needy

AFFIRMATION I feel safe within my body, mind, and heart

You have a soft, nurturing, and intuitive nature. Like the Sun rises and sets, you go through your own moods. Sometimes you may feel ready to share your gifts and messages with the world, and other times you need to retreat into your shell and spend time in reflection. Your feelings, although overwhelming at times, can become a powerful compass of guidance as you walk your life path. Trusting your intuition and learning

JUNE SOLSTICE

....

As the Sun enters Cancer, we experience the summer solstice in the Northern Hemisphere and the winter solstice in the Southern Hemisphere. The summer solstice brings the longest day of the year and the full power of the Sun. The winter solstice brings the shortest day of the year and is considered the rebirth of the Sun. The solstice is when the veil between dimensions is thin and we can access the healing power of nature with ease.

to treat your feelings as messengers will help you feel more empowered and connected to your intuition.

Along with intuition, another gift is your ability to nurture and soothe, and to lead with compassion. While this is beautiful, it is important that you also learn how to set healthy boundaries. You are a giver at heart, but when you don't have boundaries, you can quickly become depleted or find yourself feeling taken advantage of.

You are forgiving and supportive, but you need to ensure that the people in your life are respectful and are there for you as you are for them. When you don't feel loved and supported by others, you can feel lonely or feel the need to hide. If you observe this at any point, know the medicine you need is self-love. It is through this that you will find your confidence and strength to protect yourself and your well-being.

Self-acceptance and feeling at home in yourself, no matter what is happening around you, is also an important lesson. When you recognize that home is always a place within you, that is when you can feel the safety and assuredness you need to go into the world and spread your light. Take a moment to ask yourself, "Do I feel at home within myself?" Close your eyes and place your hand over your heart as you ask yourself this question. Listen to the answer that rises up. Sink deeper into this feeling and see if you can find ways to introduce this idea of feeling at home within yourself.

☉♌ | SUN IN LEO OR FIFTH HOUSE

RULING PLANET Sun

KEYWORDS confident, optimistic, creative, loyal

MOTIVATION to share your creative visions

CHALLENGES prideful, attention-seeking, sensitive to criticism

AFFIRMATION I am worthy of love

The Sun feels most at home in the sign of Leo and is able to shine and radiate at its fullest expression. This means you get to experience the true essence of our Sun, the center of our solar system, right within your own center. Having the Sun in Leo makes you magnetic. You have a sunny smile that can light up a room, and your energy is likely to be bold and memorable to those whom you encounter.

You shine brightly and may often find yourself in positions of power or leadership. One of your gifts is learning to stay positive and optimistic when you are facing struggles. You are generous, fun-loving, and may enjoy surrounding yourself with luxury.

When affection and praise are not there, you can easily feel rejected and may find yourself struggling with feelings of insecurity or needing to behave in a certain way to win the praise and affection that you crave. It is important to become aware of when you are walking this path and to remember that at the end of the day, all that matters is how you feel about yourself. Looking for external praise and reward can eventually lead you away from your true self and push you off course. Instead, aligning with your values and working toward what is important is going to lead to a far more satisfying life. Everyone will have an opinion, but the only opinion that matters is your own.

Having the Sun in Leo also indicates that your soul came for a journey of simplicity. You may find yourself wanting to seek the fanfare, but when you connect with your true values, you will find that they are far more simple and far more meaningful. Take a moment now to think about what you value most in life and see if your recent life decisions are aligned with those values. When you focus on your own desires rather than worrying about how they may look in the eyes of others, that is when you can align with your purpose.

You are as radiant as the Sun, and you need not seek approval from others in order to live your best life. Align with the bright, bold Sun that you are and shine your light ahead. It will illuminate the best path for you and guide you on the journey of your soul.

THE LIONSGATE PORTAL

· · · · · · · · ·

The Lionsgate Portal is activated by the Sun being in the sign of Leo the lion and the rising of the star Sirius. Revered by many ancient cultures, Sirius is considered our "Spiritual Sun." This occurs around the end of July to the beginning of August, but the energies of this portal reach their peak on the mystical 8/8 (August 8). During this time, we can plug into higher frequency energies to boost our soul energy, creativity, and intuition.

☉ ♍ | SUN IN VIRGO OR SIXTH HOUSE

RULING PLANET Mercury

KEYWORDS independent, efficient, of service, refined

MOTIVATION self-discovery through being of service

CHALLENGES perfectionist, worrier, picky

AFFIRMATION I am perfect just the way I am

You have a sharp mind and strive for perfection in everything you do. You have a serious eye for detail, allowing you to notice things that most people would overlook. This ability is your marker for success; however, you do have to be mindful of chasing perfectionism. Perfectionism is a mask for insecurity and fear. You can use perfectionism to stop yourself from truly being seen and from judgment. Often, this judgment is self-inflicted.

While it is great to strive to do your best, you need to check in and see where this striving comes from. Does it come from a place of fear? Know that your self-worth is not measured in what you achieve or how "perfect" your life seems on the outside. Being authentic and true to yourself is far more rewarding than striving for this perfect image. Learning to accept criticism and understanding that judgments from others are actually their own insecurities on display can help you stay connected with your center and independence.

Having the Sun in Virgo also gives you innate healing gifts. You may find yourself drawn to the healing arts, or you may be the one your friends call when they need advice. You have a strong intuition and your grounded, earthy energy allows you to access the wisdom of higher realms with ease. This is what ignites your healing qualities, so be sure to embrace this side of your personality and you will find a new way to thrive.

☉ ♎ | SUN IN LIBRA OR SEVENTH HOUSE

RULING PLANET Venus

KEYWORDS fair, peaceful, artistic, negotiator

MOTIVATION to see the self in others

CHALLENGES indecisive, codependent, vain

AFFIRMATION I balance my mind, body, and soul

Part of your soul mission is learning how to create balance in all areas of your life. This balance, however, is one that is born through ease. When you find yourself forcing things or pushing too hard, the scales are not going to be steady and will sway back and forth. Finding balance is about settling into the rhythm of your life no matter where it takes you.

You are a natural mediator and have a rare gift of being able to see the world through the eyes of others. You are compassionate to the struggles of others, and you often feel called to stand up for the injustices of the world. You are a peacekeeper but at times in your life, you may have to ask yourself whether the peace you are fighting for is compromising your own inner peace.

Returning your attention back to yourself is an important reminder when the Sun is in Libra. Part of your destiny is to discover new insights about yourself through the people you meet, but it's also important that you don't lose sight of yourself along the way. The people you encounter and the injustices that you feel passionate about are a mirror drawing you to go deeper so you can uncover your own blocks and the gifts that you can offer the world.

When your energy is scattered, you can find it challenging to make decisions and easy to fixate on the problems of others as if they were your own. When this happens, gently come back to yourself and remember that your true power comes when you feel aligned and whole within yourself and not when you are consumed with what other people are doing. Learning to relate and connect with others is part of your journey, and you may see this manifest in different ways throughout your life. Remember to keep finding balance between the self and other.

SEPTEMBER EQUINOX

As the Sun enters Libra, we experience the equinox. Once again, we can look to nature for clues on which way the energy is encouraging us to go. In the Northern Hemisphere, it is a time for retreat. In the Southern Hemisphere, it is a time for new life and creativity.

☉♏ | SUN IN SCORPIO OR EIGHTH HOUSE

RULING PLANET Pluto

KEYWORDS passionate, regenerative, spiritual

MOTIVATION to regenerate through life's experiences

CHALLENGES intense, brooding, suspicious, obsessive

AFFIRMATION It is safe for me to become who I really am

You are able to pick up on the subtle frequencies in your environment and are tuned in to the thoughts and feelings of others. This highly sensitive and intuitive nature can be challenging, but there are many gifts that can come from it when you learn to master it.

As you are a sensitive soul, it is important that you protect your energy through practices such as meditation and working with crystals. You may find it important to carve out time in solitude so you can be alone to sit with your thoughts and feelings.

Having the Sun in Scorpio indicates you are here on a journey of transformation. Your struggles and triumphs in this life become important tools of healing for yourself and for those around you. You may find that you have a difficult time fitting in or feeling like you belong, but be true to yourself, even if it means you don't fit in with the world around you.

As a strong and independent soul, you are not afraid to dive deep into your emotions. You have a gift of being able to face what is difficult and uncomfortable, and it's important for you to practice and strengthen this gift throughout your life. When you are unable to face the sometimes harsh truths around you, you can become obsessive or fixated. This can limit your awareness and the truth of your situation.

Part of your purpose is to keep transforming and shifting through the experiences that life sends your way. The only way to do this is by acknowledging the sometimes painful realities that greet us. By facing the truth, by not being afraid to dig through the dark, you will find that life takes on a deeper and richer meaning.

☉♐ | SUN IN SAGITTARIUS OR NINTH HOUSE

RULING PLANET Jupiter

KEYWORDS adventurous, energetic, playful, visionary

MOTIVATION to find meaning through life

CHALLENGES unreliable, overly optimistic, insincere

AFFIRMATION Infinite possibilities surround me now

You have the gift of being able to set your goals and make your mark. Sagittarius is ruled by the arrow of the archer, and as a Sagittarius Sun, you embody this energy with all your being. The arrow of the archer indicates that when you set a goal or make a decision, you have the strength and stamina to fire your arrow and chase your dream. When you put your mind to something, there is nothing you can't achieve and no adventure is too great!

You love your freedom and can really thrive when you feel free to do things your way and in your own time. For your own growth and development, it is important to push yourself out of your comfort zone. Do things that challenge you and stretch your mind to new limits. While you have your arrow aimed and your target set, remember that it's not the destination but the journey. It is the things you experience and the people you meet that make your destination worth reaching.

For you, life is all about opening yourself to new experiences. You have a curious and inquisitive mind. You are always seeking answers to the bigger questions and you have the gift of being able to see things from a higher perspective. When we go through hardships, it is difficult to see what's ahead or to make sense of our current situation. You, however, have the gift of being able to soar from above and see the truth of what is happening from a higher vantage point. This ability is linked to your soul's purpose in this life, so be sure to use it whenever you are feeling stuck or foggy about the road ahead. Viewing life this way allows you to see that the most difficult roads often lead us to the greatest growth and self-discovery. Life is a journey and your job is to experience all the colors it has to offer.

☉♑ | SUN IN CAPRICORN OR TENTH HOUSE

RULING PLANET Saturn

KEYWORDS ambitious, responsible, disciplined, self-sufficient

MOTIVATION to strive for better

CHALLENGES serious, all work no play, stubborn

AFFIRMATION I bring joy to everything I do

You thrive when you have a goal to work toward, and you love setting yourself seemingly impossible tasks and watching with pride at how you can overcome them. You thrive when you feel challenged and when there is hard work to be done, but don't forget to also make time for play and to allow your creativity to shine through. Getting too fixated on a goal or on achieving your ambitions can block you from enjoying and experiencing all that life has to offer. While having goals is a great motivation, they can also be limiting.

As a Capricorn Sun, you would do better setting intentions rather than goals. Intentions are more open-minded and leave space for the Universe to also weave its magic. Setting intentions rather than concrete goals can also keep you out of your head and shift you into what your soul desires.

Along with being incredibly hardworking and ambitious, you are wise beyond your years. The symbol for Capricorn is the sea goat, which is a mythical creature that understands the wisdom of the ocean and the mountains. This understanding of sea and land feeds your innate wisdom, but make sure you are balancing what you have learned from the ocean and from the mountains equally. Take a moment to bring this idea into your reality by thinking about what words are conjured up when you think of the ocean and the mountains. These words may provide some clues on what wisdom you need to lean into at this point in your life.

DECEMBER SOLSTICE

· · · · · · · · ·

The Sun entering Capricorn brings the winter solstice in the Northern Hemisphere and the summer solstice in the Southern Hemisphere. Many of the traditions we celebrate at Christmas, like decorating trees and hanging mistletoe, have been taken from pagan festivals honoring this solstice.

☉♒ | SUN IN AQUARIUS OR ELEVENTH HOUSE

RULING PLANET Uranus

KEYWORDS humanitarian, intellectual, group-orientated, healer

MOTIVATION to lift others

CHALLENGES impersonal, aloof

AFFIRMATION It is safe for me to pave my own way

You love bringing people together and uniting over common causes. You love to be social, but when the conversation starts to get too deep, you can find it difficult to open up and share what you are feeling. This is not because you don't have access to your feelings; rather, you are very cautious about whom you open up to.

While you are friendly and ready to guide others, when it comes to receiving that guidance yourself, it can be hard for you to feel safe and comfortable to get into that headspace. You have natural healing abilities but you may find that you are drawn to unconventional healing practices or that you like to do things your own way. You are independent and like to carve your own path in this life.

Part of your soul journey is bringing revolution and shaking up the status quo to help us all shift our perspectives and see things from a new point of view. You are often revolutionary in your approach, and that is definitely one of your key gifts. If you find yourself feeling out of alignment, think about where you may be ignoring the calls of your heart or shutting down your ideas out of fear of what other people will think.

You are here to innovate and bring these innovations to the world, so don't hold back and don't be afraid to walk the path that no one else has walked before. You're also a humanitarian at heart and you love being able to help and guide others, but make sure you don't lose sight of yourself in the process. Your compassion is not complete if it is not returned to yourself as well.

☉♓ | SUN IN PISCES OR TWELFTH HOUSE

RULING PLANET Neptune

KEYWORDS dreamy, creative, musical, intuitive

MOTIVATION to advance in consciousness

CHALLENGES victimhood, exaggerating, scatterbrain, noncommittal

AFFIRMATION I am One with the Universe

You are sensitive to the world around you and may find listening to music, creative activities, or spending time in nature to be therapeutic. The symbol for Pisces is two fish swimming in opposite directions; this represents yin and yang or the illusion of duality. In this three-dimensional world, we can see duality everywhere. We have light and dark, bad and good. But on higher planes and when we shift our consciousness to higher frequencies, we see that everything is one and the same, and it is only our judgment that creates duality.

This can be a difficult concept to wrap your head around at first, but it is the gift of your Sun in Pisces that allows you to ponder and stretch your mind in this way. It is your keen and intuitive understanding of the spiritual planes that allows you to venture into such questions. These two fish that seemingly go in opposite directions are creating a complete circle. They are a whole, they are one, and that is the oneness that you have the gift to attune yourself to.

Along with being intuitive, you also hold strong creative gifts. Giving yourself a creative outlet is important and can prevent you from getting lost in your mind. When your mind is full and you don't have a healthy outlet, your feelings tend to be all over the place and you head into a victim mentality. To prevent this, it is important that you take ownership over your life and find ways to stay grounded as you walk your journey on this Earth. While you may have big dreams and spiritual visions, your work right now is to be human, and it's important to find balance and to connect with that. Just the same, you don't want to forget your spiritual connection either, so be sure to aim for balance whenever possible.

THE LAST SIGN OF THE ZODIAC

· · · · · · · ·

As Pisces is the last zodiac sign, when the Sun reaches this point, it signifies a closure and an ending of a cycle. Regardless of our sign, we may feel this on some level in our own lives as we adjust to the energies of the new year.

TRACKING THE SUN THROUGH THE ZODIAC

When the Sun is in	I feel . . .	I am motivated to . . .
Aries (March 21–April 19)		
Taurus (April 20–May 20)		
Gemini (May 21–June 20)		
Cancer (June 21–July 22)		
Leo (July 23–August 22)		
Virgo (August 23–September 22)		
Libra (September 23–October 22)		
Scorpio (October 23–November 21)		
Sagittarius (November 22–December 21)		
Capricorn (December 22–January 19)		
Aquarius (January 20–February 18)		
Pisces (February 19–March 20)		

CHAPTER

The Moon

ZODIAC RULER Cancer
KEYWORDS sensitive, emotional, intuitive, nurturing
RULES OVER moods, emotions, ocean, relationship
with mother/femininity, intimate feelings

There is something about the Moon shining brightly in the night sky that reminds us that we are part of a much larger Universe. If you want to feel the effects of the heavens above on your life and develop a deeper relationship with cosmic energies, the best place to start is with the Moon. You can also deepen your connection and knowledge of astrology by tuning in to the phases of the Moon cycle.

THE MOON CYCLE

The Moon goes through phases, and so do we. The Moon represents our emotions and the things we need to feel emotionally secure as we move through this world. The Moon also represents our relationship with the feminine and our ability to tune in to the softer, more subtle vibrations of the world around us.

● **New Moon:** This is the beginning of the lunar cycle. Magnetic forces of the Moon draw us inward, encouraging us to sit with our emotions and the stillness of our own breath. The energy around us is most fertile, and we are able to call in what we wish to manifest through setting intentions and aligning our focus. This is also a good time for starting new projects.

NEW MOON RITUAL: SET YOUR INTENTIONS

On a New Moon, light a candle and write three things you would like to draw into your life. Fold the paper and place it against your heart. Close your eyes and breathe for a few minutes. Visualize your intentions becoming a reality. Keep your paper to look back on in six to twelve months to see how your intentions have come to life.

◗ **Crescent Moon:** This occurs a few days after the New Moon and is when we can see a thin crescent. During this phase, we can set intentions and think about what we want to draw into our lives.

◖ **First Quarter Moon:** Out of the darkness, we start to see the light, and we may connect the dots and feel more confident about a particular area of our life. This moon phase also calls for patience as we allow our intentions time to ripen.

◖ **Waxing Gibbous:** Things are crystalizing. We begin to see a deeper truth and become aware of our true thoughts and feelings. We see our intentions turning into realities.

The Full Moon is a great time for release work. Light a candle, get a pen and paper, and fill a bowl with water. Write three things you wish to release. Rip the paper into three strips, imagining that each rip symbolizes a letting go and releasing. Carefully place the first strip into the candle flame, allowing it to burn. When it gets too hot, drop it into the bowl of water. Repeat with the remaining strips and see how much lighter you feel.

○ **Full Moon:** This is the peak of the moon cycle. The magnetic pull of the Moon helps draw things out of us, and we may feel ourselves cleansing repressed emotions and releasing all that no longer serves. This is also a time when what we planted on the New Moon comes into full bloom.

◑ **Disseminating Moon:** As the Moon reduces in fullness, we increase our awareness and develop greater clarity around areas of our lives that feel foggy. We may receive intuitive guidance and wisdom from our higher self.

◑ **Last Quarter Moon:** We enter a stage of reflection. We can look back to the past and see how it has shaped us, but we can also look ahead and create space for the new beginnings set to arrive as the next lunar cycle begins.

● **Balsamic Moon:** We feel a new beginning on the horizon, but we may not sense exactly what is to come. We feel a need to slow down and complete projects to create space for the new.

The sign that the Moon was in at your time of birth can also give insight into your emotional personality and what you need to feel secure within yourself.

SUPERMOONS

· · · · · · · · ·

Supermoons occur when the Moon comes closer to Earth. During a Super Full Moon or a Super New Moon, the lunar energies are stronger, allowing us to access them with greater ease.

☽♈ | MOON IN ARIES OR FIRST HOUSE

KEYWORDS confident, adventurous, independent, reactive

MOTIVATION to be the leader of your life

CHALLENGES heated emotions, easily frustrated, egocentric

AFFIRMATION There is nothing I can't handle

You have the courage to speak your mind and share your truth. You need a lot of stimulation and love trying new things and seeking out new adventures. There is a tendency for your emotions to go from zero to ten pretty quickly, and this may result in you doing or saying something you may regret later. To create ease with this, learn to manage your emotions before they become too overwhelming. If you do find yourself feeling overly emotional, physical activities such as deep breathing, exercising, and so on can be a healthy way to release.

You have a natural confidence and inner strength that helps fuel your determination and drive. You feel confident and secure when you are in control and free to do things your way. In your heart you know the way and you know what is right for you, your life, and your body, so be sure to trust your inner wisdom. To connect with this inner wisdom, tune in to your breath. Gently ask yourself, "What is the most supportive thing I can do for myself?" Listen to what answer floats up and be sure to follow through.

While your independence is a strength, know that you don't always have to go it alone. Learning to accept other people's support and listening to their ideas can create balance and open you to new depths of wisdom and understanding.

☽♉ | MOON IN TAURUS OR SECOND HOUSE

KEYWORDS dependable, consistent, nurturing, romantic

MOTIVATION to find stability

CHALLENGES releasing control, fixation, letting go

AFFIRMATION I am grounded in who I am

You crave stability and comfort, and you are in touch with your heart. You like things organized and can feel anxious when there are abrupt changes you have not had a chance to digest and prepare for.

When change throws you off balance, be patient with yourself and bring your awareness to the present moment, rather than allowing yourself to get fixated on the past. You can sometimes find yourself stuck ruminating on things, so be sure to give yourself a healthy outlet by acknowledging the past, forgiving it, and letting it go.

Holding on to old pains can block your energy flow, and you may find yourself overspending, overeating, or overindulging. When you find yourself going down this path, it means it's time for you to go within and figure out what is hiding beneath the surface. Try journaling using a prompt such as "I am feeling . . . " and see what comes to the surface. Getting in touch with the truth of the heart is often what you crave. Trust the wisdom of your heart and listen to its messages so you will know the way forward.

☾♊ | MOON IN GEMINI OR THIRD HOUSE

KEYWORDS thinker, creative, storyteller, thoughtful
MOTIVATION to express and share
CHALLENGES disconnecting, gossiping, overanalyzing
AFFIRMATION It is safe for me to share how I feel

It is all too easy for you to get into your head when it comes to your emotions, rather than learning to feel your emotions from the heart. By getting into your head, you can protect yourself from feeling and experiencing the emotion. Over time, this can create a disconnect between your body and your emotions. If you find yourself unable to express emotions, it may be because you are processing them through rationalizing. To truly process and shift through your emotions, allow them, especially the more challenging ones, to move through your body.

Next time a heavy emotion comes, see if you can lean into that feeling without resisting it. It may feel intense at first, but within a few seconds, you will feel the emotion pass as a wave. Although you do have the tendency to "think" through your emotions, you are also creative and a natural storyteller.

Part of your gifts in this life is learning how to inspire others through your own authentic self-expression. Writing poetry and journaling can also be powerful outlets that can help you tune in to your emotions and digest them. When you explore your emotions on a deeper level and grow in self-awareness, you can help unlock your intuition, allowing you to pick up messages from higher realms.

☾♋ | MOON IN CANCER OR FOURTH HOUSE

KEYWORDS soft, nurturing, intuitive, sensitive
MOTIVATION to feel at home within the self
CHALLENGES boundaries, moody, needy
AFFIRMATION I love and accept myself

The Moon feels most at home in the sign of Cancer, so you may find yourself extra sensitive to the cycles of the Moon. The Moon can be your compass and a power source of energy, so tune in to its rhythms and see how you can work with it. You are empathic and have the gift of being able to pick up emotions from the world around you. While this makes you beautifully sensitive and intuitive, it is important to also have boundaries and to regularly protect your energy from harsh environments or people who tend to take advantage of you. Learning to stand up for yourself and say no to others is a valuable lesson.

You are naturally nurturing and a giver at heart. Giving and looking after others can make you feel secure and add to your feelings of safety, but make sure that you aren't overdoing it to the point of sacrificing yourself. What you can give to others, how much others need you, and how far you can bend over backward are not measures of your worth. You are worthy, so don't use your compassionate nature as a way to mask your insecurities. If ever you need the reminder, simply gaze into your eyes in the mirror and repeat aloud "I love myself" until you feel the truth of the words.

Just like the Moon goes in phases, you may find yourself feeling moody at times and needing to retreat into your shell for alone time and to recharge your batteries. Regularly practicing self-love and acceptance is key and can help you to tune in to the powerful healing and nurturing gifts that having the Moon in Cancer can bring.

☾♌ | MOON IN LEO OR FIFTH HOUSE

KEYWORDS easygoing, creative, generous, fun
MOTIVATION to shine for the world to see
CHALLENGES perfectionism, approval-seeking, dramatic
AFFIRMATION I am proud of who I am

You are easygoing and positive when it comes to your emotions. When you do get upset, it can feel overwhelming, and the fiery, dramatic nature of Leo energy can shine through. To feel safe and secure, you need to feel loved, heard, and seen. You sometimes crave recognition and praise, and you want to know that you are making a difference. You want to know that you are loved, and that what you are doing matters.

While it is always nice to receive praise and compliments, the only opinion that matters is the opinion you keep of yourself. Practicing self-love and learning how to become your own biggest champion are valuable lessons for you. You have a lot of inner strength and confidence, so be sure to connect with this and remember that you can do anything you put your mind to. You are creative, and you may find yourself drawn to working in the arts or using your creativity as an emotional outlet.

You are an expressive soul, but your true light can shine even brighter when you trust and respect yourself and the people you surround yourself with. Honesty and loyalty are extremely important to you, so even though you can be easygoing and generous, make sure you set boundaries when it comes to those you allow close to you. To embrace your vibrant Leo Moon, be sure to make time for creative activities and allow your feelings to direct your work.

☽♍ | MOON IN VIRGO OR SIXTH HOUSE

KEYWORDS sensitive, healer, thinker, logical
MOTIVATION to understand
CHALLENGES overthinking, anxiety, perfectionism
AFFIRMATION I relax and lighten my body

You are sensitive to your emotions and the emotions of others, but you have a way of thinking them through to find ease and calm. This is definitely a gift, and you may find that those around you are drawn to asking for your advice. This ability is also one of the reasons why those with the Moon in Virgo are often considered healers. When you learn to master your emotions, you have a way of processing and digesting them so they turn into powerful jewels of healing and wisdom.

You have to be mindful of overthinking or getting too caught up in your head. Replaying things in your mind is never going to serve you or give you the answers you are seeking. If you find yourself doing this, it is important to give yourself an outlet to release and let go of repetitive thoughts. You may also find yourself prone to worrying and anxiety, so try to remember to soften, let go, and focus on what is in your control.

Practices like journaling or bringing your awareness to the present moment can help, especially when you find yourself getting stuck in repetitive thinking. A quick way to bring yourself to the present moment is to observe seven things in the room that stand out to you. This exercise instantly brings your awareness into the here and now.

While it's fine to strive for your best, you tend to hide your insecurities behind perfectionism. Focusing on progress rather than perfection is a good way to shift this mindset. As you get more comfortable with your emotions, you will be able to tune in to the incredible healing qualities that the Moon in Virgo can bring.

☽♎ | MOON IN LIBRA OR SEVENTH HOUSE

KEYWORDS diplomatic, balanced, compassionate
MOTIVATION staying true to yourself
CHALLENGES projecting, indecisive, people pleasing
AFFIRMATION I am connected to all the Universe

You are diplomatic, fair, and have the unique gift of being able to see things from other people's perspective. When you are out of balance, this ability to put yourself in other people's shoes may make it difficult for you to return to your own. If you keep focusing on what people around you are doing, it is eventually going to distract you from what is happening inside of you.

If you want to change the world, it starts with yourself, and the same applies when it comes to how you process your emotions and handle your relationships. By bringing focus back to yourself, rather than projecting onto others, you can feel more decisive and connect deeper with your own true center.

You have the tendency to take on the emotions of others, so returning to the self will help you discern what emotions are your own and what burdens of others you don't need to carry. If you do find yourself taking on another's emotions, try cleansing your aura through meditation or by taking a bath with salts and essential oils.

Knowing who you are and learning to collaborate rather than compromise are valuable lessons. You may also feel called to stand up against injustices and for people who don't have a voice. Although you are a fighter for justice, equality, and fairness, make sure you treat yourself with the same principles that you so freely give to others.

☽♏ | MOON IN SCORPIO OR EIGHTH HOUSE

KEYWORDS deep, psychic, sensitive, intense
MOTIVATION transforming emotions
CHALLENGES secretive, dark, obsessive
AFFIRMATION I align with my inner power

Your piercing gaze can make people feel like you are peering into the pit of their soul, and they wouldn't be completely wrong. You have a keen and sharp intuition and are likely to hold natural psychic gifts.

You tend to feel comfortable digging through those deeper, darker emotions. You are not afraid to go there, for you know that when you sit and become comfortable in the uncomfortable, that is when you are able to shift and transform your emotions into new understanding. You have to be mindful of allowing your emotions to become consuming or spiraling into crisis mode. While you are in tune with your thoughts and feelings, it can be difficult for you to express what you are going through to others.

You tend to hide how you feel from others, and people may accuse you of being secretive. It is not easy for you to trust and open up to others, because you are so sensitive and you tend to feel things deeply. Having this shell of protection around you is important, but be mindful of guarding yourself so tightly that you find it hard to create genuine connections with others.

As you have a strong intuition and are sensitive to your environment, you may benefit from working with crystals or wearing a protective amulet. When you learn to protect your own energy and follow your intuition more, you will be able to access the transformative powers that having your Moon in Scorpio can bring.

☾♐ | MOON IN SAGITTARIUS OR NINTH HOUSE

KEYWORDS open-minded, philosophical, independent
MOTIVATION seeking new meaning
CHALLENGES opinionated, not taking responsibility
AFFIRMATION What I seek is within

You are adventurous, playful, and always looking on the bright side. As you become more in tune with your emotions, you may also find yourself feeling philosophical or digging deep to find the meaning behind your emotions and behaviors. Reading, traveling, or learning something new can be a wonderful way to take a break from any stressful or anxious emotions you may be experiencing.

As Sagittarius is a fire sign, having the Moon here can make you bright and energetic, but it can also make you prone to exaggerating versions of the truth or not taking responsibility for your actions. Like all fire signs, while your emotions can rise up quickly, they can also pass just as quickly. You have an optimism and a positive, can-do attitude that can be infectious. You love to feel good and you have the motivation to go out there and make productive changes whenever you feel down.

To feel safe and secure, you need to be free to express your true thoughts and feelings. At times you may be accused of oversharing or offering your opinion when it's not wanted. You can create healthier relationships by balancing your desire for freedom while still taking into account the emotions and feelings of others.

☾♑ | MOON IN CAPRICORN OR TENTH HOUSE

KEYWORDS practical, wise, moral, responsible

MOTIVATION to use emotions as tools of growth

CHALLENGES insensitive, dismissive, ruthless

AFFIRMATION I choose to feel joy

While others may get caught up in waves of emotion, you have a way of seeing past that and getting right to the heart of things. This ability is definitely helpful, but you need to be mindful of dismissing your emotions and how you are feeling. All feelings are valid, deserve to be heard, and can be powerful clues to the inner workings of your soul.

Letting down your guard, allowing yourself to connect with compassion, and being vulnerable will help you create a deeper relationship with yourself and others. You are good at staying surface level with your emotions; however, there are real gifts to be had if you can push past any fears or resistance and dive deep into the truth of your heart. When you feel safe to navigate your true feelings and sit with the wisdom and knowledge that you gain, you can use it as a powerful compass to help you navigate through your life.

To feel secure, you like to have long-term goals to focus on and strive for. Keeping a vision board or a list of goals in your room can be a soothing and inspiring reminder for you. You crave success and are highly ambitious, just don't forget to enjoy the ride.

☾♒ | MOON IN AQUARIUS OR ELEVENTH HOUSE

KEYWORDS eclectic, humanitarian, healer

MOTIVATION to find the greater good

CHALLENGES dismissive, insensitive, opinionated

AFFIRMATION I practice compassion

You are a pioneer and don't subscribe to the tried and true. You like to pave your own way and do things to the beat of your own drum. You tend to speak your mind and have the natural ability to see what is needed for the greater good. While this makes you a wonderful humanitarian, it can also leave you prone to ignoring or dismissing the needs of those closest to you. What is good for the group is not always good for the individual, and being sympathetic and aware of this may sometimes be necessary.

Aquarius is the sign of the water bearer. The water bearer is able to collect the heavier emotions of the world and transform them into lightness before returning them to Earth. You have this natural ability when it comes to others, but it is important that you also practice this on yourself. Getting in touch with your emotions will help you unlock these natural healing gifts and will also connect you to greater compassion. You may also find baths, chanting, or music to be a source of healing for you.

To feel secure, you crave freedom and the ability to do things at your own pace and in your own way. You enjoy your own company, and while you are friendly and warm, it's likely only a few people get to know the true you.

☽♓ | MOON IN PISCES OR TWELFTH HOUSE

KEYWORDS intuitive, musical, spiritual, compassionate

MOTIVATION to turn feelings into inspired action

CHALLENGES victimhood, self-absorbed, overly sensitive

AFFIRMATION I believe in myself

This is a highly intuitive placement, so you are likely to be in touch with your own emotions and the emotions of the world around you. It is important for you to learn how to process your emotions in a healthy way so they don't consume you or leave you feeling overwhelmed.

Due to your sensitivity, you may find spending time in nature, listening to music, or doing creative projects a good way to help you release and let go of any emotional stress you may be carrying. Sitting with your breath or listening to the waves of the ocean can also be extremely soothing.

Your sensitive and emotional nature can sometimes lead you prone to feeling like a victim or becoming self-absorbed. It is important to recognize when you are doing this so you can shift your thinking and find new ways to empower yourself and expand your mindset. When you learn to master your emotions in a healthy way, you can unlock the psychic, intuitive, and creative gifts of your Pisces Moon.

WORKING WITH THE MAGIC OF THE MOON

NEW MOON
Bring fresh energy
into your life

CRESCENT MOON
Take steps to manifest
your goals

BALSAMIC MOON
Retreat and reflect

FIRST QUARTER MOON
Be open to change

LAST QUARTER MOON
Release and let go of the past

WAXING GIBBOUS MOON
Surrender and trust
the process

DISSEMINATING MOON
Give yourself closure

FULL MOON
Claim your power and
allow yourself to shine

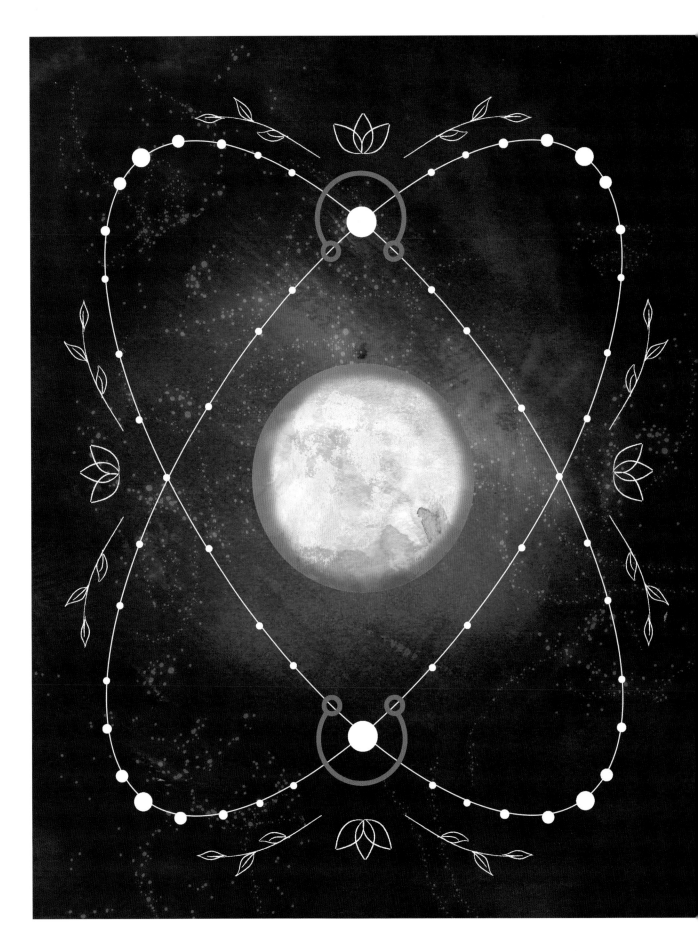

5

Your Lunar Nodes

The lunar nodes are technically not planets but a mathematical point calculated between the Sun and the Moon. We have both a north and a south node that lie directly opposite each other. These points indicate the karmic debts of our past and what our soul has come to achieve in this incarnation. The zodiac signs of the nodes also indicate the signs that we will experience the eclipses in.

☊ | NORTH NODE

The north node indicates the core lesson of your soul through this lifetime. The path to finding the lessons of your north node begins with your south node. Your north node is where you are heading, and the south node holds the clues for how to get there.

☋ | SOUTH NODE

Your south node indicates the lessons that you mastered in your previous incarnations. As you have already mastered these things, if you live or operate from your south node, you could have feelings of stagnancy and a lack of growth. The idea is to embrace your south node talents and skills and use them to pave the way for your north node destiny.

THE LUNAR NODES AND ECLIPSES

The current placements of the lunar nodes indicate the zodiac signs that the eclipses will fall in. There are two types of eclipses: a solar eclipse, which falls on a New Moon, and a lunar eclipse, which falls on a Full Moon. We typically have four to six eclipses per year, and in astrology, eclipses are incredible transformational points. They indicate a portal between one state of consciousness and the next. Eclipses often bring recognizable change and transformation in our lives, especially when they line up with our personal lunar node sign.

By understanding the sign and houses your nodes were in at the time of your birth, you can see the core messages of your soul's blueprint come together. The lunar nodes spend about eighteen months in each sign, so while the zodiac carries some personal significance, it also carries a generational influence.

☊♈ | NORTH NODE IN ARIES OR FIRST HOUSE/
☋♎ | SOUTH NODE IN LIBRA

In previous lifetimes, you lived a life of service and were always attending to the needs of others. While this is one of your most valued traits, in this life, you need to learn the art of collaboration, rather than compromising how you think and feel.

Part of your lessons in this life is learning how to be independent rather than letting others make decisions for you. You may fall into people-pleasing tendencies, which can leave you feeling stuck. Real growth comes when you learn it's safe to express yourself. Find your inner warrior, stand firm, and become the leader of your own life.

☊♉ | NORTH NODE IN TAURUS OR SECOND HOUSE/ ☋♏ | SOUTH NODE IN SCORPIO

In previous lifetimes, you were always helping others to succeed and get ahead. You were a support to those in powerful positions, and it was your keen eye and incredible observation skills that helped them make it to the top. In this life, your purpose is to learn how to build yourself up and to go after your own dreams and wishes. Rather than looking outside of yourself for validation and praise, you need to learn how to create it from within. You need to be your own biggest champion and support in this life.

While we all need support from those around us, you thrive and shine when you are able to find your independence and know your true self-worth. You are worthy; you deserve to have a good life. As long as you don't believe this, you are constantly going to find yourself being held back or crushed by the opinions of others. This life is a journey in establishing your self-worth and confidence, taking all you did for others in previous lifetimes and doing the same for yourself—because you are worth it!

☊♊ | NORTH NODE IN GEMINI OR THIRD HOUSE/ ☋♐ | SOUTH NODE IN SAGITTARIUS

In previous lifetimes, you were a traveler, wanderer, and spiritual seeker. You lived a life of solitude and preferred to go wherever the wind would take you. In this life, you have come to take all of this wisdom and knowledge and learn how to integrate it into your everyday life. You need to take all your ideas, thoughts, and feelings and learn how to ground them in reality and in how you choose to express yourself.

Part of your purpose is also learning how to be social and how to integrate and work with others. In previous lifetimes, you often did things alone, but now you need to learn how to interact and get along with others. You have a lot of wisdom to share in this lifetime, so find the confidence to share your incredible knowledge with the world.

☊♋ | NORTH NODE IN CANCER OR FOURTH HOUSE/ ☋♑ | SOUTH NODE IN CAPRICORN

In previous lifetimes, you held positions of great responsibility. You were a leader and in charge of organizing and running everything. You had a lot of weight and pressure on your shoulders, and many depended on you. In this life, however, you have come to let all of that go. While you had to learn in previous incarnations about being dependable and taking responsibility, in this life, you have come to take a more nurturing approach. This doesn't mean you need to ignore the lessons of your previous lifetimes; rather, you need to build upon them by finding a sense of balance. When it comes to your responsibilities in this life, know that you don't have to do it alone. It's okay to ask for help and it's okay to share the burden with others. Part of your purpose in this life is learning how to nurture and take care of yourself and others.

In previous lifetimes, perhaps it became easier to do your job if you could see things in black and white, but in this life, that approach is no longer going to serve you. You are here to explore all of your emotions and to connect with the voice of your heart. Your mind is a powerful tool, but it becomes more powerful when you learn to connect it with the wisdom and intelligence of your heart.

☊♌ | NORTH NODE IN LEO OR FIFTH HOUSE/
☋♒ | SOUTH NODE IN AQUARIUS

In previous lifetimes, you spent a lot of time surrounded by others and focused on the needs and well-being of the group. Your mind was always racing ahead, as it wasn't only your needs that had to be met but the needs of those around you too. It was never easy for you to make big decisions, as there was so much for you to consider.

In this life, you have come to learn how to focus on yourself and your own independence: your thoughts matter, your feelings matter, and your concerns are valid. This doesn't mean you ignore the thoughts and feelings of others; it means you don't ignore yourself any longer. You don't have to think about everyone and everything; you have to focus on what feels right for you and the rest will fall into place. Your skills and abilities from the past make you passionate, empathic, and aware of the world around you. Trust this, and know that when you are in service to yourself, it becomes easier to be in service to others.

All of the problem-solving skills you acquired in previous lifetimes are valuable, but in this life, you will find much more success and harmony when you follow your creativity instead. Part of your purpose in this life is learning how to follow your creative inspirations and use your imagination to dream up things for your life. You are allowed to have big dreams in this life, so don't limit or hold yourself back. Dream big and see where this life can take you.

☊♍ | NORTH NODE IN VIRGO OR SIXTH HOUSE/
☋♓ | SOUTH NODE IN PISCES

In previous lifetimes, you didn't like to follow the rules. You were always doing things your own way and hated to conform. You lived a creative and imaginative life and were always chopping and changing based on your mood and how you were feeling in the moment. You could get distracted easily and may have found it difficult to find something to focus your attention on.

In this life, you need to take this dreamy and creative approach and channel the energy into something focused and grounded. You need to take all of this creative inspiration built up over previous lifetimes and actually turn it into something tangible and based in the real world.

While following your intuition is always helpful, in this life, you can't afford to ignore your rational mind either. You need to make peace with your mind and learn how to use it as a formidable tool. You are also a natural healer and may be drawn to working in medicine or other healing pursuits.

☊♎ | NORTH NODE IN LIBRA OR SEVENTH HOUSE/ ☋♈ | SOUTH NODE IN ARIES

In previous lifetimes, you were the warrior and fearless leader. You were in charge of leading the pack and keeping things together when life got heated. You were extremely independent, and many looked to you for answers. This resulted in you having to wear a mask and never revealing your vulnerability. In this lifetime, you have to take down the mask and learn how to work with others.

While in previous lifetimes, you were so used to doing things alone and having to lead, in this life, you have to learn how to collaborate and work with others. You will get further in this life when you learn how to let your guard down and reach out for help and support when you are in need. It's okay to be vulnerable and expose yourself; in fact, the more you do, the more you will find yourself softening and opening to your compassionate qualities. Allowing yourself to be vulnerable helps you release shame and make peace with your fears and insecurities.

You also hold gifts in this life of being able to teach and show others how to be their own leader. Rather than trying to lead others, like you did in previous incarnations, in this lifetime, you can show others how to be leaders of their own lives.

☊♏ | NORTH NODE IN SCORPIO OR EIGHTH HOUSE/ ☋♉ | SOUTH NODE IN TAURUS

In previous lifetimes, you were organized. You liked to map things out step by step and were routine and methodical about your approach. This served you well and helped you slowly but steadily reach your goals and fulfill your dreams. You were cautious, but it was the right approach.

In this life, taking this methodical approach is going to leave you feeling stuck in a rut. You need to learn how to take a leap of faith and trust your instincts and intuition a little bit more. You have mastered slow, methodical planning, but now you need to learn how to throw out the plans and follow the music of your own life. When you do, life is going to feel far more rewarding and you are going to open yourself to so many new experiences. You grow not when you stick with what is familiar, but when you find the courage to try something new. Keep pushing yourself, keep challenging your boundaries, and keep motivating yourself to step out of your comfort zone when you find yourself getting caught up in a rigid routine.

There is a lot of success and harmony to be had when you can keep an open mind and move through life with a sense of awe and learning. You don't need to have it all figured out, so keep surprising yourself. Keep your plans in the back of your mind, but allow your intuition and the flow of life to take the lead.

☊♐ | NORTH NODE IN SAGITTARIUS OR NINTH HOUSE/ ☋♊ | SOUTH NODE IN GEMINI

In previous lifetimes, you loved collecting data and random facts. Knowing gave you a sense of comfort, and you often could be found studying, reading, and learning. Perhaps there was this sense that the more you knew, the more protected you would be as you moved through your life.

Your job in this life is to take all of what you have learned in previous incarnations and apply that to the real world. Taking action is going to be a big theme of your life, so see where this resonates for you and where you can step out of your head and into a place of action.

Along with this, you are also here to learn how to find your own truth. As you were such an avid seeker in past lives, it is important for you in this life to seek from within. Everyone is going to have their own ideas and their own way of looking at the world, but what matters in this life is that you learn to develop your own perspective.

☊♑ | NORTH NODE IN CAPRICORN OR TENTH HOUSE/ ☋♋ | SOUTH NODE IN CANCER

In previous lifetimes, you had strong ties to your family, and obligations within the home prevented you from being able to live the life you desired. Perhaps you were stuck following in your family's footsteps or perhaps you took on the role of a caregiver. This experience has helped turn you into the warm, nurturing, and compassionate person you are today.

In this life, you are being given the green light to follow your own goals and dreams. Your lesson is to learn how to cut the cords that are keeping you bound so you can take responsibility for the life you wish to lead. No one is going to do this for you; you have to learn how to step up, set your boundaries, and climb your own mountain to the top.

When you find yourself seeking answers or approval from others, check in with yourself and see if you can break this habit by recognizing the strength and determination you have within. When you set your mind to something, there is no stopping you. Think about what you want, go for it, and don't let others influence the path you take.

☊♒ | NORTH NODE IN AQUARIUS OR ELEVENTH HOUSE/ ☋♌ | SOUTH NODE IN LEO

In previous lifetimes, you were found in positions of power. Wherever you went, people noticed you and even admired you. You were the center of it all, and many gathered to help support and lift you higher.

In this life, you have come to take all of that admiration and attention you received and channel it into being of service to others. This is not to say you can't have your own ambitions and dreams, but getting to your final destination is a group effort, not a solo journey. As you lift and support others, you in turn will be lifted and supported too. There is no stepping on other people's toes or competing to get ahead in this life. That path is simply not going to serve you. As you discover ways to work and collaborate with others, you will also feel far more aligned with your purpose.

Having the north node in Aquarius also indicates that your soul has come to help usher us into the "Age of Aquarius." The Age of Aquarius celebrates this idea where all humans can live as equals and in harmony with one another. Your soul is helping pave the way for this, so tune in and allow yourself to be guided.

☊♓ | NORTH NODE IN PISCES OR TWELFTH HOUSE/ ☋♍ | SOUTH NODE IN VIRGO

In previous lifetimes, you were focused and had a laser-like approach to all that you tackled. When there was a problem or an issue to be solved, you focused on finding all the necessary answers and understanding the finest of details. This incredible ability allowed you to be well respected and trusted.

You bring this incredible talent into this life with you, but something needs to change. Rather than getting bogged down in facts and small details, you need to learn how to focus on the bigger picture and the hidden meaning within your own soul. You have come for a spiritual journey, and by getting out of your head and into your heart, you are going to see that success and harmony are much easier to find.

Sometimes your need to control can block your intuitive voice and your creative ideas. Learning to surrender and go with the flow is a far more suitable approach for you in this life. Rather than setting goals and making plans, create an intention and simply trust that the next step will arise in perfect timing.

PLANETS: THE COSMIC MESSENGERS

We are all made of stardust, and whether we realize it or not, we are connected to the entire Universe. In astrology, there are three types of planets: personal planets, gateway planets, and higher consciousness planets. Each planet holds a particular vibration and emits a frequency that we all have the capacity to feel. The sign and location of the planet at the time of your birth will color how you experience this frequency.

Your Personal Planets

MERCURY   VENUS   MARS

The personal planets make up our base personality: Mercury rules over our mind, Venus rules over our heart, and Mars rules over our ability to take action. As these planets orbit closest to the Sun, their energetic effects are more noticeable, especially on a day-to-day level. The energy of these planets can also influence and trigger us differently, depending on what we are currently going through in our lives.

CHAPTER

6

Mercury

ZODIAC RULER Gemini and Virgo
KEYWORDS communication, self-expression, thought processes
RULES OVER technology, cars, travel, moving parts, phones,
journalism/writing, nervous system

Mercury is considered the Messenger of the Gods and governs how we communicate, think, and express ourselves. Mercury is able to source messages from the gods and has access to the full potential of our mind. Mercury can help us unlock the wisdom from our soul and understand ourselves on a mental level. Its energy assists us in collecting data and coming up with ideas so we can make the best decisions for our lives. By understanding and connecting with your own Mercury, you can gain deeper insight and awareness into the inner workings of your mind.

MERCURY: THE MESSENGER OF THE GODS

Mercury is the planet closest to the Sun. In ancient mythology, it was Mercury's job to collect wisdom and insights from our life-giving Sun, which was seen as a god itself. Mercury was its closest confidant and the one responsible for receiving the wisdom of the Sun and passing it to those on Earth.

We can use this symbolism as a mirror in our own lives, with Mercury representing our mind and the Sun representing our soul or inner divinity. Clearing through the clutter of our mind can help us access the messages and wisdom of our soul.

We all come into this life with innate wisdom and insights for our life journey, but often we get lost in the noise of the world and in the noise of our thoughts, and we forget we always have the answers inside. When we learn to master our mind and thoughts, when we learn to find inner harmony with our thoughts and create inner stillness, rather than being trapped in our "monkey mind," these pearls of buried wisdom can rise into our awareness.

What type of thoughts do you keep closest to you? Your thoughts are like signals being beamed into the Universe. Your thoughts are like messages to the gods of creation. Whatever you are sending out is sent right back to you.

If you want to change your life, it all starts in the mind. While we may have no control over what comes our way, we always control how we think about it. We can either see life as a struggle or we can choose to see it as an opportunity for growth. We can either feel stuck and limited by our life, or we can see opportunities and find the gratitude for what we have.

In the outside world, Mercury also rules technology, transport, and any form of communication. If you need to sign a contract, book a flight, or buy a car, computer, or another piece of expensive machinery, it is always helpful to have Mercury in a strong position, because we can think clearly and make the decision that is best for us.

MERCURY RETROGRADE

· · · · · · · · · ·

☿ ℞ From our vantage point here on Earth, the planets can sometimes appear to be moving backward. Although this is not actually the case, when a planet does this, it is referred to as being in retrograde. Mercury retrogrades about three or four times a year.

When Mercury goes retrograde, its energy goes inward and instead of becoming that trusty messenger helping us to think clearly, our thoughts can become a little foggy and we may find we are met with delays, miscommunications, or technology breakdowns. This is a sign from the Universe that it's time to go within and reflect on the past to see if there were any messages or information we have missed along the way. We need to go back and look over the past so we can better move forward.

When we find ourselves being met with delays or mishaps under a Mercury retrograde, it is best to pause before moving ahead. Mercury retrograde also helps uncover thoughts from our subconscious mind and allows us to dig deep to gain fuller awareness. As Mercury goes through this process, we need to give things time, which is why it is best to avoid signing long-term contracts or making big commitments when Mercury is in retrograde. We need to wait for all the facts to be presented to us before moving ahead.

BORN WITH MERCURY RETROGRADE?

· · · · · · · · · ·

Being born with Mercury in retrograde indicates karmic lessons around communication and how you choose to express yourself. It can also indicate that you are a freethinker and like to pave your own way when it comes to how you choose to think about things.

Your personal Mercury sign indicates how you communicate, your state of mind, how you process your thoughts, and where you can receive the best inspiration for your ideas. You can also tune in to the different qualities of Mercury whenever it is touring one of the zodiac signs as well.

☿♈ | MERCURY IN ARIES OR FIRST HOUSE

INSPIRED BY working out, mental stimulation
COMMUNICATION STYLE direct, to the point, can be harsh

You are a fast thinker and quick on your feet. You seem to know the right thing to say at exactly the right moment, but when you are moving too quickly or not in alignment, you can lash out and say things you may regret later.

You have a sharp mind that works best when you give it the mental stimulation it needs. If you are feeling mentally foggy or overwhelmed, vigorous exercise or tackling a challenging task can be a good way to clear through the clutter and find clarity. You are full of great ideas and may find yourself starting lots of projects. Be mindful of biting off more than you can chew or committing to things before you understand what is involved.

Your mind can be the birthplace for visionary ideas, so be sure to follow through on the ones that resonate with you the most.

☿♉ | MERCURY IN TAURUS OR SECOND HOUSE

INSPIRED BY rest, contemplation
COMMUNICATION STYLE slow, deliberate, stubborn

You are a methodical, practical thinker but sometimes you can get stuck in repetitive thought patterns. You may find it hard to let things go or you overanalyze things with such detail that it makes it hard for you to move forward. Learning to trust the flow will help with this, as will breaking down problems into smaller, more manageable steps.

You have sharp focus, just make sure you are focused on the things you wish to be attracting into your life and not the things you don't. Your mind works best after a good night's sleep and plenty of rest, so be sure to prioritize your sleep schedule and make time to rest and recharge.

Your mind is always thinking of ways to build, strengthen, and make things better— and this is the gift you can offer to the world.

☿♊ | MERCURY IN GEMINI OR THIRD HOUSE

INSPIRED BY journaling, sharing ideas, reading
COMMUNICATION STYLE conversational, curious, asks lots of questions

Mercury is most at home in the sign of Gemini, so this placement indicates harmony and strong gifts when it comes to communication. You have a sharp mind, strong intellect, and seamless way of taking facts and information from the world around you and presenting it into organized thoughts. You always know the right questions to ask, and your inquisitive mind always ensures you are going to get to the bottom of things.

While you are blessed with a sharp mind, it can also run into overdrive, turning into a jungle of anxious, repetitive thinking. Getting your thoughts on paper and learning to slow your mind through meditation will help keep your mind clear and bright.

Your mind is the birthplace of storytelling, and this is the gift you can offer to the world.

☿♋ | MERCURY IN CANCER OR FOURTH HOUSE

INSPIRED BY alone time, familiar environments
COMMUNICATION STYLE tender, forgiving, sensitive

Your emotions can get in the way of your thoughts and make it difficult for you to think clearly. When this occurs, it is best to take time to pause and deal with your emotions first. Once the heaviness of the emotion passes, you will find it easier to tune in to the wisdom of your logical mind.

You do your best thinking when you are comfortable. That comfort can come when you are alone, but it can also come when you are in a familiar environment surrounded by those you love and care about. You can be a private person, so having a strong support system where you feel safe to share how you feel is important. Learning to stand up for yourself and not allow your emotions to cloud your judgment are valuable lessons for you in this lifetime.

Your mind is the birthplace of nourishment and support. Make sure you are offering this gift to those you love—and to yourself as well.

☿♌ | MERCURY IN LEO OR FIFTH HOUSE

INSPIRED BY creative projects, being heard

COMMUNICATION STYLE loud and proud, honest, confident

While Mercury is all about the mind, for you, it is the mind–heart connection that is important. When your heart and mind are in balance, that is when you feel the best and can think with the most clarity. Balancing the heart and mind means acknowledging your feelings, your thoughts, and the voice of your intuition. It is about finding a way to honor and feel your emotions *and* understand where they come from so you can better make sense of how they may be motivating or guiding you.

Turning to creative projects and allowing your thoughts room to breathe can help create stillness and clarity when you are feeling overwhelmed. You also have the natural ability of being able to lead and guide others; stand up for yourself and find your confidence, and your words will flow with ease.

☿♍ | MERCURY IN VIRGO OR SIXTH HOUSE

INSPIRED BY mental stimulation, organizing

COMMUNICATION STYLE thoughtful, practical, creative

Mercury is ruled by the sign of Virgo, providing you with a real harmony and flow when it comes to how you communicate; however, you can be prone to perfectionism or worrying about every little thing. Be sure to find balance when this happens, and focus on being mindful rather than moving through life with your mind full.

Buried under perfectionism is often fear: the fear of not being good enough or not being accepted. Remember, Virgo is ruled by the strong and independent virgin. Here, the word *virgin* represents a strong and independent person who doesn't need a partner or anyone else to define them. When you claim your own independence, you will be reminded of how capable and worthy you are.

☿♎ | MERCURY IN LIBRA OR SEVENTH HOUSE

INSPIRED BY collaborating with others

COMMUNICATION STYLE fair, rational, indecisive

You like taking a balanced approach when it comes to tackling your mind. A list of pros or cons and weighing your options are things that you may find helpful too. While you like to ponder all that is on offer, sometimes too many options can leave you feeling fatigued. You may feel a struggle with what the "right" thing is to do and find yourself feeling stuck in the process.

Learning to trust your intuition can help you make quicker and more thoughtful decisions, and it can stop your mind from running into overdrive. It is also worthwhile to remember all decisions, whether we label them as right or wrong, eventually lead us to where we need to be. Making the "right" decision is making the best choice with what you currently know and feel, and trusting that no matter what comes your way, you are strong enough to make it through.

☿♏ | MERCURY IN SCORPIO OR EIGHTH HOUSE

INSPIRED BY divination, nature, introspection

COMMUNICATION STYLE intense, reserved, poetic

If there is something lurking in the shadows of your subconscious, you have the natural strength and curiosity to venture deeper to bring it into the light. You are not one for small talk, and you need to feel like you are in a safe environment before you can share and express your truth. When you don't feel safe, you might withdraw back into the watery depths of your poetic mind.

You have a creative way with words. When you do feel confident to open up and share, you can drop pearls of wisdom that those around you were not expecting. At times you can get wrapped up in the intensity and the seriousness of your thoughts, so be mindful of this and make sure you are creating space for lightheartedness and play.

☿♐ | MERCURY IN SAGITTARIUS OR NINTH HOUSE

INSPIRED BY traveling, learning, teaching
COMMUNICATION STYLE outspoken, motivational, direct

You love to look on the bright side of things and have a natural gift for motivating your-self and those around you. When you get clear with what you are feeling and thinking, and point yourself in the direction of your choosing, you can allow life to flow. When you lose your sense of direction, when you get caught in your mind, you find it much harder for your arrow to reach its target. The trick here is learning to get in touch with the voice of your heart and how you are feeling. Get clear and still with your heart, and you will always know which way to aim your arrow.

You love to feel free to express yourself, but when it comes to offering your opinion, sometimes it is better to keep it to yourself unless you have been asked. Giving yourself an outlet such as journaling or a creative project can be a great way to allow thoughts to flow freely and can prevent you from oversharing.

You have a mind that is thirsty for knowledge, so make sure you are constantly learning and trying new things.

☿♑ | MERCURY IN CAPRICORN OR TENTH HOUSE

INSPIRED BY researching, fact-checking
COMMUNICATION STYLE practical, blunt, honest

You have a natural ability to see things from a practical point of view, but it is also important to recognize that we don't ever truly see things as they really are; instead, we see things the *way we are*. Our past experiences, our judgments, the way in which we view the world are always coloring our experience of what we see. What is black and white to us may appear that way through our limited experience. Part of your journey in this life is learning to clear outdated ways of thinking by remaining open-minded. What you once believed may not necessarily fit with who you are today, so be open to new ways of interpreting your thoughts and your life experiences.

Integrity and ethics are important to you, and you are always on the quest for a deeper truth. Don't forget to zoom out so you are not missing the bigger picture. When your mind is feeling full and you are in need of a release, researching can be a comfort. Read advice from experts or people who have gone through the same situation, or research something different to get your mind off whatever is troubling you. Your mind is a sharp tool, just ensure you are keeping it open and not allowing yourself to get fixated on outdated thoughts that no longer serve who you are today and who you want to be.

☿ ♒ | MERCURY IN AQUARIUS OR ELEVENTH HOUSE

INSPIRED BY being independent, trial and error
COMMUNICATION STYLE inclusive, technical, soothing

You are a freethinker and highly innovative. You have a different way of seeing the world and are always looking in the opposite direction of whatever way the wind is going. Don't doubt yourself. Although you have a way of thinking that is out of the box, there is often wisdom to be gained from allowing yourself to explore this.

Part of your purpose in this life is learning how to do things differently and to challenge the status quo when it comes to how you think about things. It is through walking this path of fearless self-expression that will draw you closer to your true self and your destiny.

When your mind is full and cluttered, you may find it soothing to think about how you can turn your attention toward helping others. Sometimes, the best way to get out of our own heads and the chaos of our own lives is by asking, "What can I do to help others?" It is through helping others that you also help yourself.

☿ ♓ | MERCURY IN PISCES OR TWELFTH HOUSE

INSPIRED BY music, retreat
COMMUNICATION STYLE flowery, heartfelt, indirect

Your mind is full of daydreams, and you may find it difficult to keep your thoughts rooted and grounded in your present reality. You have an abstract way of thinking about things. While others may be able to trace things from A to B, you like to explore a greater territory and see things as more open-ended and less direct. Sometimes, what you are thinking and feeling cannot be expressed into words. It is almost like words won't do it justice or the right words don't exist to explain what you are thinking and feeling. At times, these deep, ethereal thought processes make it difficult for you to concentrate or focus on the task at hand. You may also find it hard to express to others what you are thinking and feeling in a simple way.

To support you on this journey, your intuition will be your guide. While you may struggle to "think" your way through life, you most definitely have the ability to "feel" your way through life, and this can become your superpower. Your soul is here to express its abstract, dreamy, and creative thoughts, so allow yourself to wander, just make sure you don't get lost there. Return to the present as often as you can and recognize the value in the here and now.

CHAPTER

Venus

ZODIAC RULER Taurus and Libra
KEYWORDS beauty, femininity, love, divine, intuitive
RULES OVER relationships, money/profits, fashion,
beauty industry, creative work

Venus is the planet of love, beauty, romance, creativity, and money. Venus energy is magnetic and is attuned to the vibration of our heart center. Whenever there is a matter involving the heart, we can look to Venus for clues and guidance. Along with being a guiding compass for our heart, the sign Venus was in at the time of our birth can signal what we need to feel emotionally fulfilled, what we are attracted to, and what we value.

Venus typically spends four to five weeks in each zodiac sign; however, like the Sun and the Moon, Venus has its own cycle, which takes about eighteen months to complete. The cycle of Venus begins with Venus as a morning star: Morning Star Venus. At this time of year, Venus can be seen rising along with the Sun. Over the course of nine months, Venus starts pulling away from the Sun and ends up as a bright evening star that we can see clearly.

Venus as a night star, or Evening Star Venus, is the boldest and brightest in the sky! But about nine months later, this bright evening star dips below the horizon. This represents the "death" phase or retrograde phase of Venus. When Venus disappeared from the night sky, the ancients believed it had slipped into the underworld. In the underworld, Venus would tend to the heart wounds we have not yet cleared or dealt with. If we have old pains and resentments, they can come up to the surface to be cleared and released during this retrograde period.

After a few weeks, Venus emerges from the underworld and is now a morning star again. This is known as the rebirth of Venus and is a time when we can feel our heart energy being reborn. Like Venus, we are ready to begin a new cycle and uncover a new layer of our heart's wisdom and truth.

Venus as a Morning and Evening Star

Morning Star Venus represents the outer self of the goddess. It is an energy of giving, compassion, and outer beauty. Evening Star Venus represents the inner expression of the goddess. It is an energy of receiving, self-love, and inner beauty.

You can check your birth chart to see if you were born under a Morning Star Venus or an Evening Star Venus. Here's how:

Locate your Sun and Venus on your chart. Look to see what sign they are in. If Venus is located at an earlier zodiac sign to your Sun, then you have a Morning Star Venus. If Venus is at a later zodiac sign to your Sun, you were born under an Evening Star Venus.

For example: Sun in Aquarius (eleventh zodiac), and Venus in Capricorn (tenth zodiac). Venus is in an earlier zodiac sign, so this is a Morning Star Venus. Or, Sun in Libra (seventh zodiac) and Venus in Sagittarius (ninth zodiac). Venus is in a later zodiac sign, so this is an Evening Star Venus.

If your Venus and Sun signs are in the same sign, you will need to look at the degrees. If your Venus is at a lower degree than your Sun, you are a Morning Star Venus. If your Venus is at a higher degree than your Sun, you are an Evening Star Venus. If they are at the same degree, you are also a Morning Star Venus.

If you were born with Venus as a Morning Star, you are here to work on your inner qualities of self-love, self-compassion, and learning to trust yourself. If you were born with Venus as an Evening Star, you are here to work on your outer qualities of giving love and compassion to others, and learning to trust others.

The Rose of Venus

As Venus and Earth orbit the Sun, they do a dance with each other, creating a perfect pentagram or five-petal flower, which takes eight years to complete. This geometric pattern is known as the Rose of Venus. Each petal is said to represent a different quality of Venus's energy and our own growth in consciousness as we journey through the rebirths of Venus. As Venus is connected with the heart chakra, we can meditate on this beautiful geometric pattern to help open and unlock our heart. Gaze at the image above for five to ten minutes and write whatever comes to your mind. You may be surprised what heart messages are revealed to you.

Our heart is the birthplace of our intuition and our creativity, and it is our source and connection to the love that we are. By charting the energies of our Venus sign and working with the cycles of Venus, we can understand our heart and what it needs as we navigate through this life.

♀♈ | VENUS IN ARIES OR FIRST HOUSE

LOVE IS passionate, at first sight, physical

You are fiery, passionate, and tend to fall in love fast! While you can always trust the wisdom of your heart, be mindful not to rush too quickly into things before you are certain.

You know what you want. Once you make up your mind, it can be hard to convince you otherwise. You have confidence when it comes to putting yourself out there and telling others how you feel. People are drawn to you for your independence and your innovative way of approaching life.

Part of your journey in this life is learning to stand true in who you are and to embrace your more fiery qualities. While you don't want to burn things, you also don't want to dim your light to make others comfortable. Surround yourself with people who respect who you are and can handle your bright inner flame.

♀♉ | VENUS IN TAURUS OR SECOND HOUSE

LOVE IS trust, respect, richer over time

Venus loves being in the sign of Taurus, so this energy flows harmoniously. You have Venus energy at its best and are highly magnetic. You have the gift of drawing things to you like a moth to a flame, so be careful what you wish for!

While Venus is the planet of love and beauty, it is also the planet of money. Venus in Taurus indicates that your relationship with money is significant for you in this lifetime. If money were your partner, how would you rate the quality of your relationship? Creating a healthy relationship with money is part of your purpose in this life.

Taurus is also associated with self-worth, so this placement can indicate a need to open yourself to receiving the gifts and bounties of the Universe without allowing yourself to get trapped in thoughts of scarcity or that you are not good enough. Focusing on gratitude will help appease this, so whenever you notice the voice of fear or doubt creep in, acknowledge it, but also look to what you feel grateful for.

♀♊ | VENUS IN GEMINI OR THIRD HOUSE

LOVE IS fun, being connected, being heard

This is a fun and flirty placement! Venus in Gemini loves to talk, ask questions, and make the other person the center of attention. Talking and connecting on a conversational level is what can light up sparks with those you meet. Communication is important in all relationships, but for you it can also be the key to your heart. When you feel heard, when you feel the other person is listening and caring about what you have to say, that is when you feel the safest to let your guard down and allow others in.

When you are feeling insecure or defensive, your Gemini twin can rear its head and pretend you are unfazed or not bothered. We all have masks, but know that putting yourself out there and being vulnerable is a sign of true bravery!

You are a master with words, but you also need to be careful of promising more than you can offer or saying one thing but doing another. Make sure your words are aligned with the truth of your heart and you will always feel in balance.

♀︎♋ | VENUS IN CANCER OR FOURTH HOUSE

LOVE IS giving, compassionate, safe

You are soft, sensitive, and cautious with love. You are heart-driven and tend to feel the emotions of the world, so learning how to open your heart even wider can be a delicate matter.

As you are so sensitive, you can trust your intuition and your first impressions when it comes to meeting people. If something feels off, it often is. As you are so sensitive, opening up and sharing with others can feel challenging, but know that as you follow your intuition and get confident with yourself, you can make those connections more easily.

Part of your purpose in this life is learning how to feel safe and secure within yourself. The more confident and secure you feel inside, the easier it will be for you to open up to others. While self-love is an important lesson for all of us, for you, learning to love yourself is key if you want to be able to learn to love others. While receiving love is important, when Venus is in Cancer, the lesson of self-love is very pronounced.

♀︎♌ | VENUS IN LEO OR FIFTH HOUSE

LOVE IS exciting, passionate, intense

You are highly creative and fun-loving. You are always seeking pleasure, and you know how to have a good time. You are charming and have a dazzling smile that can light up a room! You have a magnetic aura, and you are likely to find that people are drawn to you for your good vibes and your ability to always have a good time. You have a great sense of humor and may often be the center of attention in every room you walk into.

There is no doubt this is a magnetic and attractive placement. Part of your purpose in this life is allowing yourself to shine and not feeling the need to dim your light. Boost your confidence and learn to be comfortable in the spotlight. Share your heart energy and creative wisdom with the world, as it will lead you to success.

♀♍ | VENUS IN VIRGO OR SIXTH HOUSE

LOVE IS independence, healing, intuitive

You are independent, and it is important for you to be connected to the truth and wisdom of your heart at all times. Part of your purpose is learning to stand in your own truth and follow your own heart's calling, regardless of what others may be doing around you. You have a strong heart center, but in this lifetime, your flame burns for you! You deserve to channel all your passion and love into your personal projects and what excites and calls to your spirit.

On a soul level, you have lots to do in this life, and you would be best suited to a partner who can acknowledge this and support you as you do your work. While you have an independent soul, know that it's okay to ask for support when you need it. There is no shame in this. While you are here to use your heart wisdom to bring your creations to life, you can't do it all alone.

♀♎ | VENUS IN LIBRA OR SEVENTH HOUSE

LOVE IS togetherness, peaceful, working as one

Venus loves being in the sign of Libra, so this energy flows harmoniously and effortlessly. How you relate and connect with others is an important soul journey for you in this life. The people closest to you are important teachers for you. Even the people who challenge you and rub you the wrong way have lessons to teach and share with you.

Those around you can be like a mirror, helping you understand your own triggers and your own truth. While we may seem like we are separate individuals, on a soul and energetic level, we are all connected, we are all One. We are all in this together, and learning to work with others, no matter how different they may be from you, is all part of your journey. Learn to see yourself in others, but also learn to stay true to yourself and your individual spark.

♀♏ | VENUS IN SCORPIO OR EIGHTH HOUSE

LOVE IS intimate, private, intense

Intimacy and physical touch are important to you in your relationships and are a part of how you build your connections with others. While you are a romantic at heart, you are also a private person, and it is not always easy for you to put yourself out there and open up.

Not opening up and sharing how you feel can make you a little obsessive or fixated, making you more stuck or confused about what to do or say. Try not to let it get to that stage by finding the confidence to share how you feel or to approach whomever you are interested in. This takes courage, so tune in to that brave Scorpio energy and know there is no harm in trying!

When you do feel safe to open your heart, you can feel love intensely. Make sure you are keeping yourself grounded. Part of your purpose in this life is learning to evolve and become more of your true self through the lessons and journeys of your most important relationships.

♀♐ | VENUS IN SAGITTARIUS OR NINTH HOUSE

LOVE IS friendship, growth, inspirational

You have a bright, friendly, and bubbly personality. You may find many are attracted to your laugh, your smile, and your easygoing attitude. You are attracted to people with big ideas and think differently about the world. You are a traveler and an explorer at heart, and you need someone who is going to be open and willing to take this journey with you. You may find you are drawn to connecting and forging relationships with people who have a different culture than your own.

While you love to be around people, you crave your independence and freedom. You need to feel like you are free to roam and free to do things your own way and in your own time. You have a strong life direction and purpose, and you don't need anyone getting in your way! Staying focused on your own path and finding a partner who is supportive of this is important for your journey in this life.

♀♑ | VENUS IN CAPRICORN OR TENTH HOUSE

LOVE IS supportive, patient, better with time

You love to be in relationships where you can share your goals and dreams and support each other as you both climb your own mountains. Success is highly appealing to you, and ambition can be a great motivator for you in this life, just don't forget to keep tuning in and listening to the wisdom of your heart. Your heart speaks as a soft whisper, and it is connected to how you are feeling, rather than what you are thinking.

You can have the tendency to ignore the feelings of your heart in favor of your rational and practical mind, but know that there are gifts to be had when you can learn to embrace the more wavy qualities of your emotions. Don't be afraid to dive deep into your emotions, and don't feel the need to justify or rationalize them away with your thoughts. You are here on this journey to learn how to feel, to allow yourself to experience a rainbow of emotion, so don't rob yourself of that. Connecting deeper with your emotions will help you forge meaningful connections with others.

♀♒ | VENUS IN AQUARIUS OR ELEVENTH HOUSE

LOVE IS freedom, empathy, generous

You have a big heart and are drawn to helping, supporting, and lifting up others. You are caring and have a way of looking out for everyone. While you love to give and be around others, you also crave your freedom and don't want to feel like you are being held back or tied down by anyone.

While you are a people person, you can feel a little exposed when it comes to opening your heart or being in the spotlight of a conversation. You are good at asking the questions, but not so good at answering them when they are asked of you. To enter into deeper, more committed partnerships, you need to learn how to let down your guard and allow yourself to receive. Because you are so good at giving and supporting others, make sure there is an equal balance of give and take in your relationships. When you are feeling heavy in your heart or overwhelmed by your emotions, you may find that being of service and helping others can lighten your load.

♀♓ | VENUS IN PISCES OR TWELFTH HOUSE

LOVE IS spiritual, for all, truth

You are highly creative and in tune with the intuitive wisdom of your heart. You are romantic and sensitive, and you are interested in relationships that allow you to connect on the deepest of levels. While you are fine engaging in small talk, what interests you and makes you feel attracted to another is when you can dive deep and explore the feelings and emotions bubbling beneath the surface.

You are connected to your heart, which means you are sensitive to your emotions and the emotions of others. These empathic gifts can be a great tool to help ignite your intuition, but they can also leave you feeling drained. Make sure you are protecting your energy by setting boundaries and surrounding yourself with people who respect you and have your best interests at heart.

Part of your purpose in this life is learning to connect with your creativity, intuition, and spirituality. Merging the three can help activate your passions and open your heart center even wider.

· · · · · · · · ·

If Venus is within 5 to 7 degrees of your Sun, rising, or Moon sign, it indicates you are highly magnetic, attractive, and creative! We all get a taste of this energy when a transiting Venus—that is, the current position of Venus in the zodiac—comes to touch these areas of our chart. You can figure out where Venus is by using an Ephemeris or any astrology app or software that offers the current positions of the planets (see the Resources on page 170 for more guidance). Use this powerful Venus this energy to your advantage by working on creative projects, connecting with your heart, and scheduling beauty treatments.

VENUS COMPATIBILITY FOR LOVE AND FRIENDSHIP

Your Venus Sign	Most Compatible Venus Signs
Aries	Aries, Leo, Libra, Scorpio, Sagittarius
Taurus	Taurus, Virgo, Libra, Scorpio, Capricorn
Gemini	Gemini, Virgo, Libra, Sagittarius, Aquarius
Cancer	Cancer, Scorpio, Capricorn, Pisces
Leo	Aries, Leo, Sagittarius, Aquarius
Virgo	Taurus, Gemini, Virgo, Capricorn, Pisces
Libra	Aries, Taurus, Gemini, Libra, Aquarius
Scorpio	Aries, Taurus, Cancer, Scorpio, Pisces
Sagittarius	Aries, Gemini, Sagittarius, Leo
Capricorn	Taurus, Cancer, Virgo, Capricorn
Aquarius	Gemini, Leo, Libra, Aquarius
Pisces	Cancer, Virgo, Scorpio, Pisces

♀

CHAPTER

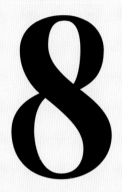

8

Mars

ZODIAC RULER Aries and Scorpio
KEYWORDS taking action, motivation, inner warrior,
impulses, ambition, competition
RULES OVER wars/weapons, energy levels,
sex, surgery, accidents

Mars is the warrior planet that exudes a fiery passion. Its energy helps us take action in our lives, and it keeps us motivated and following the path that makes us feel alive and filled with purpose. Where Mars was at the time of your birth can indicate where you express your most energy, where you feel most motivated, your passion, and what drives you in this life. It can also indicate your inner warrior and how you face the battles and struggles that life brings your way.

MARS: THE FEARLESS WARRIOR

Mars was named after the God of War, and there is a rich symbolism here that can help us unpack the nature of this planet's energetic vibration. As the planet of war, Mars was fearless. It knew it would come up against obstacles, enemies, and challenges, but it was armored and ready to handle whatever life threw its way. Mars would also ride a chariot drawn by two horses, Phobos and Deimos, meaning fear and panic. These horses are also the names of the moons of Mars. Mars would ride into battle with its two horses, instilling fear and panic. This fear and panic helped Mars conquer kingdoms and win violent fights.

Mars is definitely a fiery and sometimes hotheaded planet. It rules our heavier emotions such as fear and panic, as well as anger, frustration, jealousy, and betrayal. Mars energy can make us feel hostile, but this is because it tunes in to our personal fears. When we are in a fearful state, when we feel panic inside of ourselves, we can feel insecure, easily threatened, jealous, and frustrated. It is our own fear and panic that can make us start a war with ourselves and with the events that greet us on our life's journey.

While Mars is the God of War, there is a different way we can approach this energy. Rather than allowing our fears to get in the way, we can instead use them as powerful tools of motivation. Rather than squashing and hiding our fears so they manifest as insecurities, we can ride with them, confidently, and bravely, into whatever life has in store for us. One reason Mars is such a fine warrior is because it has dealt with its fear. It isn't hiding away from its fear; rather, it is riding with it. When we acknowledge our fear, that is when we can make peace with it, and like Mars, we can use our fear as a clue as to which way we need to ride.

Our fear is there to protect us and keep us safe, but it is what we fear that indicates where we may have blocks when it comes to achieving and getting where we want to be. Acknowledging our fear allows us insight into the deepest desires of our soul. Take a moment to get still with yourself and write your three biggest fears. Don't judge yourself. See if you can create some ease with what you have written. Sometimes the best way to soothe a fear is to honor that it is there.

THE CYCLE OF MARS

Mars takes twenty-three months to orbit the Sun and spends about six to eight weeks in each sign. As Mars reaches the end of its twenty-three-month cycle, it also reaches the fullest point of its energetic potential. It is at this point that Mars will turn retrograde and begin moving through its own process of "death and rebirth." When a planet turns retrograde, its energy is drawn inward and we are encouraged to use it on an inner level rather than an outer level.

As Mars is the planet of action and energy, a retrograde period can make us feel slow and sluggish, but it is also a time for us to check in and ensure that we are not burning ourselves out. When Mars goes retrograde, we can use it to take a breather from our busy lives and think about whether our actions are aligned with what motivates us. As Mars moves out of retrograde, we feel rejuvenated and reborn, ready to tackle a new cycle. While we all feel this Mars Cycle, we also have our personal Mars Cycle that we can track.

YOUR MARS CYCLE

The Mars Cycle begins when Mars returns to the same spot it was in at the time of your birth. This is called the Mars Return, and it occurs approximately every twenty-three months from your time of birth.

The Mars Return: This six- to eight-week period is a time of high energy for you. You will feel extra motivated, energetic, productive, and on your game. You are driven during this period and have the strength and stamina to move mountains. You may find new projects coming your way with ease, or you may find you are called to take on more responsibility. This is also a great time to conquer those fears and to make ambitious plans for the future.

The Mars Opposition: This is when Mars enters the opposite sign from where it was at the time of your birth. This happens about one year after your Mars Return. During this six- to eight-week period, you may feel sluggish and depleted. You may need to slow down, retreat, and catch up on extra sleep. You may notice your fears being highlighted or coming to the surface to be cleared.

As Mars moves away from the opposite sign and heads back toward its return, you may feel the need to release things and projects from your life that have served their time. As you approach your Mars Return again, you will have more space for new and exciting projects that are a better match for your energy.

While you have your natal Mars to work with, you can also tune in to the many messages of Mars as it makes its way through the zodiac.

BORN WITH MARS IN RETROGRADE?

♂℞ If you are born with Mars in retrograde, you need to make an extra effort to access your Mars qualities. However, this extra effort is only until you find what works for you. You need to find your own motivation and way of doing things. What drives you is not going to be aligned with the status quo. It will be easier for you to access your Mars energy once you learn to follow your passions and what motivates you.

An ephemeris is a log of all the planets and what degree of the zodiac they are in. You can get it as a book or as a digital version online. Find more information in the Resources section on page 170.

♂♈ | MARS IN ARIES OR FIRST HOUSE

MOTIVATION to create and lead others

Mars loves being in the sign of Aries and can express its fiery, passionate, and energetic qualities to the fullest. Having Mars in Aries gives you a strong motivation and willpower to do things and to act. You always have ideas bubbling away in the back of your mind, and it's your strong and powerful Mars that helps you make the leap from idea to action. This is an energetic placement, so make sure you are giving yourself an outlet to express this energy.

When you feel depleted or burnt out for prolonged periods, it could be because you are expressing your energy in a way that is not fulfilling to your true self. Your Mars needs stimulation, but the right kind of stimulation. Think about how you can bring more energy into your life, focusing on your passions and the things that light a fire inside of you. You are a born warrior, so make sure you are tuning and tapping in to that innate strength you were born with.

♂♉ | MARS IN TAURUS OR SECOND HOUSE

MOTIVATION slow and steady wins the race

Taurus likes to move slowly and methodically, whereas Mars wants to move quickly and act! This can create a feeling of restlessness, where you may feel caught up between jumping in to take action and waiting for the right moment to act. Sometimes in life, there is no such thing as the right or perfect moment. Sometimes you have to step up and take the plunge to lead you to the next chapter of your journey.

While you want to look before leaping, be mindful of overthinking it or getting so stuck in indecision that it prevents you from moving at all. Finding balance between thinking things over and taking that leap of faith is an important life lesson for you. While you may feel indecisive, you are also patient and have the strength and stamina to go the distance. While others may lose steam, your methodical approach sees that eventually you will always get to where you need to be. Taking small, consistent steps can bring great rewards in time.

♂Ⅱ | MARS IN GEMINI OR THIRD HOUSE

MOTIVATION think your way through

You are always asking questions and trying to get to the bottom of things. Your mind moves quickly, and you want to extract the information you are looking for and move on to the next thing. While this may be favorable at work, you may need to learn to slow down in your personal life and learn to savor the time you share with others.

You thrive in busy environments and feel best when you can have your hands in multiple projects at once. It can be difficult for you to stay focused on one thing for a long period, so having some diversity can help you stay motivated and on track. Be mindful of spreading yourself too thin or overcommitting to projects. When you become overwhelmed, it can be harder for you to keep your focus and get things done, so only say yes to things you want to do.

♂♋ | MARS IN CANCER OR FOURTH HOUSE

MOTIVATION make love, not war

In Cancer, the warrior is not interested in fighting or pursuing war; instead, it wants to go home. It wants to return to what is comfortable and safe, and yet, when it does, it cannot express its fullest qualities. You may feel a struggle between being the free, independent warrior ready to conquer the world and being safe at home in your comfortable surroundings. When you are in the world, you want to be home, and when you are actually home, it can be difficult to express your true self and honor all that you know to be true about the world you have seen.

To balance this energy, you need to learn how to be independent while also honoring your feelings and need for security. You need to learn how to create a comfortable environment in the home that makes you feel safe and welcomed. You need to have somewhere soft and cozy to land, for when you do, you will feel more confident and comfortable taking risks in the outside world.

♂♌ | MARS IN LEO OR FIFTH HOUSE

MOTIVATION self-belief

The Mars in Leo warrior sets out to battle feeling confident—and extremely well dressed, too! While it may not be the best warrior on the field, Mars has confidence that sets it apart from the rest. Whether you think you can or you can't, you are probably right. And that is the motto of Mars in Leo. By believing in yourself and knowing you can, there is nothing you can't achieve.

Your confidence is your strong point, so make this work for you. If finding your confidence is difficult, look back to your childhood at who you were before the world told you who you should be. How fearless were you? If you align with your authentic self, you can find your confidence and live for yourself rather than for others. Connect with that fire of passion burning inside of you and ride off on your gallant and beautiful horse. Your confidence and willpower bring you all the luck and success you need in this life.

♂♍ | MARS IN VIRGO OR SIXTH HOUSE

MOTIVATION independence

The warrior in Virgo is independent and doesn't need help. It knows what it wants and how to do it, and it doesn't need other people getting in the way. It wants to be free and independent to do things its own way. The Mars in Virgo warrior has a precise plan and knows every move it will make down to the second. No one else could understand this level of precision, so it is better to go it alone.

While a lot can be achieved in this way and there is success to be had, learning to work with and trust others to help you can be more effective. There are lessons to be had through going it alone, and sometimes life will call for this. But it's also important to learn how to reach out for help and support when needed. While your vision and plan may be perfect, sometimes it is worth giving up this perfection to connect or make memories with others. There is no doubt you have the strength and tenacity to fight any battle single-handedly, but just because you can doesn't mean you should.

♂♎ | MARS IN LIBRA OR SEVENTH HOUSE

MOTIVATION justice for all

The warrior in Libra never wants to choose sides; it wants to talk things over and find a peaceful and fair resolution that will make everyone happy—but this rarely can make everyone happy. As the saying goes: you can please some of the people some of the time, but you can't please all of the people all of the time.

While being the peacekeeper is a valiant skill to have, learning when to step back and not involve yourself in other people's problems is also a good skill. It is not always your job to play the middle and figure out how to satisfy everyone. While you want to keep the peace, it is your inner peace that is most important. As you move through your life, you may be challenged in this area. But, as you get more comfortable and confident in your own skin and learn to connect with your truth, it will become easier for you to put your inner peace first and foremost. Use your gifts to keep the peace, but don't do it at the sacrifice of your own.

♂♏ | MARS IN SCORPIO OR EIGHTH HOUSE

MOTIVATION inner knowing

Mars loves being in the sign of Scorpio and feels free and confident to express its energy to the fullest. The warrior Mars in Scorpio is thrifty, a little manipulative, and always thinking ten steps ahead. Rather than rushing into battle, the Mars in Scorpio warrior is carefully calculating its next move and knows what others will do, maybe even before they do! You are clever and cunning and have the mind of a brilliant chess player. You are also a natural detective and can see things many others would miss.

While you are good at spotting the clues, you are good at hiding them too. You can be secretive and may not wish to let on to others how you are thinking and feeling. You can be a closed book, but when you learn to trust yourself, it's easier to trust those around you. Letting your guard down and allowing yourself to be vulnerable can also grant you access to a new set of skills, ones that are more intuitive and even psychic. Don't close off to the wisdom of your heart. While your mind is so sharp, your heart can help you see things that even the mind can miss.

♂♐ | MARS IN SAGITTARIUS OR NINTH HOUSE

MOTIVATION freedom

The Mars in Sagittarius warrior likes to run with the wind. It knows when the battle is and what time to be there, but it is anyone's guess whether it will actually show up! There are bigger concerns, and distractions, laid along the path that simply must be experienced. While Mars in Sagittarius can sometimes be unreliable, there is a strong urge to go with the flow of life and not miss out on the random and exciting opportunities you encounter along the way.

Keeping a certain level of spontaneity in life can relieve feelings of stagnancy, and while it's beautiful to stop and smell the roses and follow the callings of life, be mindful of making promises you can't keep or committing to more than you can handle. You need a certain level of freedom, but you also need structure and routine to get things done. Honor your desire to do things your own way and in your own time, but be sure to take responsibility and create boundaries for yourself. The Sagittarius warrior can thrive with boundaries, as long as there is an open door.

♂♑ | MARS IN CAPRICORN OR TENTH HOUSE

MOTIVATION ambition

Mars loves being in the sign of Capricorn for it can use the ambition and drive of the sea goat to climb mountains taller and reach destinations faster. The Capricorn Mars warrior knows how to lead. It has the wisdom and experience but also the stamina to make it to the other side of whatever battle or hurdles are laid in its path. While others may give up, the Capricorn warrior is relentless and will continue until it has reached its destination.

Success is a driving motivator for you in this life. When you put your mind to something and want to achieve it, there is nothing you can't do. You are driven and motivated, just make sure you are stopping to enjoy the journey and not just the destination. You can get in the habit of chasing the goal without giving thought to the steps you have to take to actually get there. If you don't enjoy the journey, is the destination still worth it? Only you can be the judge of that.

♂♒ | MARS IN AQUARIUS OR ELEVENTH HOUSE

MOTIVATION helping others

The Mars in Aquarius warrior leaves no one behind. It wants to work as a team and ensure that everyone is well equipped and prepared for whatever challenges may greet them. The Mars in Aquarius warrior loves to lead but wants to do so in a way that serves the greater good and not just themselves. They lead to be of service to others and not the other way around.

The Aquarius warrior is a true team player and is always looking out for others. While it is a noble thing to support and lift up others, it is important that you don't lose sight of yourself along the way. Being there for others is so much part of your calling, but if you are not there for yourself, if you are not looking after your own needs, there is no way you can truly give to others. It is your inner spark, your inner juice, that is so valuable and helpful to others, but you can't pour from an empty cup. Work on filling yourself so you overflow, and from that overflow, doing the work and sharing the message of your soul.

♂♓ | MARS IN PISCES OR TWELFTH HOUSE

MOTIVATION ease

The Mars in Pisces warrior has battled in many wars, but now it realizes life is not about being at war or charging uphill to get where it wants to be. Don't be at war with yourself any longer: that is the message of Mars in Pisces. This energy is about surrendering to the flow of your life and allowing things to be as they are, rather than fighting them. This doesn't mean you can't make changes or make different choices, but allow these choices to come from a place of ease rather than a place of struggle.

We can spend our whole lives fighting the suffering and confronting of our inner demons, or we can simply say, "This is who I am. This is my story, and rather than fight it, I will just accept it." It is okay to make mistakes, and it is okay if things aren't perfect. Staying present, staying in your awareness, and allowing yourself to be as you are can be a powerful way to instigate positive change and bring ease.

The Gateway Planets

JUPITER   SATURN

The gateway planets are the bridge between the personal planets and the planets of higher consciousness. These gateway planets are Jupiter and Saturn along with the asteroid Chiron. These celestial bodies begin taking us from our outward personality into the deeper depths of our inner personality. By walking the bridge that the gateway planets provide, and working through the lessons and gifts they offer, we can step into a higher state of being and elevate our consciousness to new levels of awareness and enlightenment.

Jupiter

ZODIAC RULER Sagittarius
KEYWORDS abundance, expansion, opportunity
RULES OVER fame, fortune, law, higher education,
religion/philosophy, international travel

Jupiter is the largest planet in the solar system and has a strong magnetic force that can help expand our mind, our heart, and the opportunities around us. Our Jupiter can also indicate natural strengths and talents, and where we are given an extra sprinkling of luck. Jupiter reveals to us where we can thrive and shows us the areas of our lives where we may find we have natural gifts and talents.

JUPITER: BRINGER OF ABUNDANCE

In ancient times, Jupiter was considered the Supreme God whose presence shined a light and revealed a deeper and more awakened truth. Jupiter's energy has the power to help us see the bigger picture. When we see the bigger picture, we gain a new level of clarity to see how all events eventually lead us to where we need to be.

As we navigate through our lives, we can get stuck in the day-to-day routine and caught up in our problems and the struggles that greet us. But when we zoom out, we see things differently. Stepping back gives us new perspective and allows us to see the inner workings of everything unfolding. We can see that there is always some divine plan unfolding and that life has a deeper meaning and purpose that is not always easy to understand when we are caught up in our own lives. When we see the bigger picture, we can give meaning to the things that happen in our lives, and we can see how one event that we may have labeled "bad" actually led us to some of the more amazing opportunities and gifts that life has offered us.

Jupiter's presence gives us this silver-lining awareness. It helps us arrive at knowing that there is a purpose for all things that fall in our path. We can look to see where Jupiter was when we were born for clues on where we may find our greatest success and abundance in this life.

JUPITER RETURN

Jupiter spends at least twelve months in one sign of the zodiac, but when it returns to the sign it was in at the time of your birth, this is special and is known as your Jupiter Return. Your Jupiter Return occurs when transiting Jupiter returns to the exact degree of the zodiac it was at the time of your birth. This happens every twelve years, so an easy way to figure out when you are having your Jupiter Return is to think about how old you are. At age twelve, we experience our first Jupiter Return, then the next occurs at twenty-four, then thirty-six, and so on. Jupiter Return is a significant period in our lives that indicates a time of awakening and seeing the bigger picture.

At your first Jupiter Return, you are coming into your teenage years and the curtain is pulled back, revealing more to life or more to adulthood than first imagined. See if you can think back to what was happening around the age of twelve and what significant events stand out to you.

The next Jupiter Return at age twenty-four is usually more significant. At this time, another piece of this picture is revealed to us. We are excited about the new opportunities on offer to us, but we may also have to look at the current state of our lives and figure out whether we really want what we are pursuing.

JUPITER RETROGRADE

······

♃ ℞ Being born with Jupiter in retrograde indicates you have the ability to bring luck, abundance, and success to those around you. Through giving to others, you find your own way to success too. As you support and lift up those around you, you are able to tune in to more of the gifts behind your natal Jupiter. Jupiter retrograde can also indicate that part of your soul purpose is to unlock the buried treasures that are nestled within you. You came into this life with a lot of wisdom, and as you dig deeper, you will be able to uncover these nuggets of wisdom to guide you on your journey.

Jupiter then checks in with us again every twelve years, revealing a little more of the picture and allowing us to sink a little deeper into who we are. Jupiter also brings new opportunities and gifts, and it helps us unlock hidden talents. A Jupiter Return lasts for twelve months, so when you are turning a multiple of twelve, keep track of what lessons and offerings Jupiter may be bringing your way.

Now, let's consider Jupiter through the zodiac. Remember, you can always tune in to this energy when Jupiter is in a particular zodiac sign.

♃♈ | JUPITER IN ARIES OR FIRST HOUSE

GIFT independent self-starter

It's time to roll your sleeves up and get to work! Jupiter in Aries indicates your soul is here to bring a fresh new start to your life in some way. Part of your journey is learning how to trust your ideas and innovations and take the first steps to bring them into reality. Don't worry about having all the answers; sometimes starting first then seeing where you end up is the approach to take. Your gifts and talents lie in your ability to command respect and lead others. You do well when you are in charge, and you have a way of organizing those around you to be more productive and efficient.

While you are direct and can see the path clearly ahead, be mindful of closing your mind off to the ideas of others. Staying open-minded can help keep you aware of the opportunities and doors the Universe is opening for you.

You have a strong energy and a great enthusiasm for life. You know what you want, so trust yourself and know there are no limits on what you can achieve. This is an energy of new beginnings, so don't be afraid to start things over as you outgrow or find that the old ways are no longer working for you.

♃♉ | JUPITER IN TAURUS OR SECOND HOUSE

GIFT steady success

The planet of expansion can expand far and wide in the sign of Taurus, but it takes its time. This is a slow and methodical expansion, not a loud and fast one. As you trust yourself and learn to open your heart wider, you will see your life in new and more interesting colors. As you expand yourself and your life experiences, life around you will expand as well.

While Taurus likes things to remain stable and consistent, Jupiter encourages you to move, keep trying new things, and not stay in one place for too long. In this life, it is all about finding a balance between these two energies. While it is fine to remain where you are and find your comfort zone, eventually you are going to need to break free from it if you want to keep expanding and shining your light bigger and brighter for the world to see.

When was the last time you did something new for the first time? Doing new things can feel scary, especially as we get older. As adults, we get so used to doing things that feel familiar and comfortable and that we know we are good at. But when we do this, we are not learning or expanding our horizons. Even though trying something new can feel intimidating at first, make it a point to challenge yourself a few times a year by learning a new skill or trying something new. Keep your safe comfort zone, but give yourself permission to explore and change things up too.

♃♊ | JUPITER IN GEMINI OR THIRD HOUSE

GIFT thoughtful communication

Your mind is the birthplace of many thoughts and ideas! You have a sharp, intelligent mind and this is where your power lies. You have so many thoughts and ideas that learning how to take charge and managing the contents of your mind are going to be necessary skills. Practices such as meditation are wonderful for learning to tame the mind and clear your thoughts, but you may also like to try something more active, such as journaling, especially first thing in the morning or last thing at night.

As your mind is strong, it is important that you keep it stimulated with the right kind of input. Monitoring your thoughts and ensuring that they are not self-limiting or self-deprecating is important for everyone but especially for you. Creating a beautiful and peaceful mental state is something that is going to serve you well and will allow you to access the gifts and power of your mind.

You also have natural skills and talents when it comes to working with your hands. You are good in all areas relating to communication. With a clear mind, you will be able to find the solution to every problem and to every struggle that greets you on this life journey.

♃ ♋ | JUPITER IN CANCER OR FOURTH HOUSE

GIFT compassionate protector

Your kind eyes and compassionate heart are your secret weapons. While people are drawn to your warmth, part of your journey in this life is learning how to fill your cup with self-love and nourishment. You are giving and are always thinking of ways to help others, but your purpose in this life is learning to give to yourself too. You need to embrace the idea of receiving, and the main thing you need to learn how to receive is your own love, compassion, and forgiveness.

Can you look at yourself in the mirror and say "I love you"? How easily can you forgive yourself when things go wrong? You are already a being of love, but your task lies in learning to open to the love that you are. Your task is to remove all the blocks and boundaries you have created that keep love out of your own heart. You have a lot of love to give in this life, not just to yourself but to others as well. While everyone deserves to receive love, be mindful about who you are choosing to allow in your presence. Sometimes loving from a distance is okay.

♃ ♌ | JUPITER IN LEO OR FIFTH HOUSE

GIFT creative confidence

You are here to share your message with the world, but there are a few speed bumps to watch for along the way. As your soul innately knows that it has a message to share with others, it can lead you to crave attention or feel like your journey needs to be extra special and unique compared to others. We all have our own unique paths to walk in this life, so be mindful of disregarding the journeys of those around you.

You carry a strong wisdom in your heart and when you learn to tune in and connect with it, you will always feel guided and protected. Leading your life from the heart is something you are gifted at doing, but if you have forgotten or are unsure of what it feels like to lead from your heart, take a moment to tune in. Place your hand over your heart and breathe here for a moment, feeling your heart energy. Connect to what your heart is feeling right now and listen to what arises. What you hear is the sound of your heart connecting and communicating with you. Keep practicing this heart communication and eventually it will strengthen with time. Your heart holds the key to your life, so make sure you are connected and listening to its wisdom.

♃ ♍ | JUPITER IN VIRGO OR SIXTH HOUSE

GIFT natural healer

While Jupiter wants to look at the bigger picture, Virgo wants to focus on the details—and this can create a conflict when it's not kept in balance. There is a clarity to be found by seeing the bigger picture, but there is also a clarity that can come from looking at the smaller details. When you learn to find balance with both these viewpoints, that is when you can tune in to your gifts and talents a little more.

The next time you find yourself getting fixated on something and caught up in the details, see whether you can allow a little more room for the bigger picture to emerge. And just the same, the next time you are focused on the bigger picture, see whether you can zoom in a little bit so you are not missing any of the important details.

You also have the innate and natural gift of being able to rebuild yourself after hardship and trauma. You are a natural healer, and no matter what challenges come your way, you always have the ability to work through them and rise up stronger. You have the natural gift of being able to put the broken pieces back together, not just in your own life but in the lives of others too.

♃ ♎ | JUPITER IN LIBRA OR SEVENTH HOUSE

GIFT understanding others

As Jupiter reveals more of the picture, Libra is looking to see how it can fit what it sees under the label of good or bad. However, with Jupiter's ability to keep expanding to reveal more of the picture, this can be an endless quest. As more information is revealed, the more we change our awareness of what is good or what is bad. We may think something bad has happened or we have been treated badly, but with greater awareness, we are able to see how that bad or negative event may not have been about us, or may have led to a path of higher destiny. It is not possible for things to always be labeled as good or bad; it is only our judgment that says it is so.

While we cannot put things into compartments, we can trust and see that balance is always achieved. It is a law of nature. When something ends, something else is born. When a door closes, another opens. This is nature and the laws of the Universe in action. Part of your purpose is learning how to find more wholeness. It is about learning to stop judging or getting caught up in what's good or bad, and just allowing yourself to stay present with whatever life brings your way without feeling the need to label it. You are always entitled to feel what you feel, but see whether you can allow yourself to feel without judging that feeling as well. When you learn to bring more acceptance to your life and move out of judgment, you will unlock more of your blessings and gifts that this life has to offer you.

♃ ♏ | JUPITER IN SCORPIO OR EIGHTH HOUSE

GIFT strong intuition

Jupiter shines the light on areas of our lives that have felt shadowy or dark. It exposes the truth and can help us see things that were tucked and buried away in our subconscious so we can heal and shift them once and for all. Scorpio is that darkness. Scorpio is that process of tucking things away into the dark corners of our mind and heart in order to look at when the time is right.

As you have Jupiter in Scorpio, your shadows don't remain hidden for long. While other people can get away with leaving their shadows in the dark for the rest of their lives, you cannot. It is part of your purpose in this life to keep shining a light on your shadows so you can shift and move past them. While you may try to bury your pains, traumas, and truthful feelings, they will never stay hidden for long. Jupiter is always there, ready to shine its light and expose them so they can be transformed once and for all.

All through your life you may feel you are on this journey of peeling back the layers you have surrounded yourself in, to find a deeper truth. Sometimes it may feel like the layers will never end, but eventually you will get to your core, to the root of who you are, and from this place you will be able to access your greatest gifts.

You were blessed with the powers of transformation. You know how to take the darkness and shine your light on it. You know how to honor what the darkness is trying to show you, but you also have the awareness that the darkness is no place to stay. We all must visit there from time to time, but we have to keep returning to the light over and over again. It's a process, but each time you make the journey, you are advancing your soul and the souls of all the planet.

♃ ♐ | JUPITER IN SAGITTARIUS OR NINTH HOUSE

GIFT positive mind-set

Jupiter is ruled by Sagittarius, so it feels most at home here and it's able to express its energy to the fullest. When Jupiter is in Sagittarius, it is a rebirth moment. This is the time that Jupiter is bathed in a new and restorative light and is lifted to its highest frequency and vibration.

You have this wonderful, optimistic, and abundant energy on your side to guide you as you make your way through this earthly journey. With Jupiter in Sagittarius, you are motivated and are always looking on the bright side when it comes to achieving your goals. You are always looking for ways to open your mind and open your heart to life and the experiences it brings your way, and you are always seeking that next great adventure.

As you fill your life with rich and rewarding experiences, you are able to keep sinking deeper into who you are and what fills you up in this life.

Part of your journey is learning how to return to joy, and you can achieve that by quenching your curiosity for life and all it has to offer. Don't be afraid to keep searching and exploring new experiences. Just keep in mind that it is also important to stay grounded and keep a sense of routine and structure. You are a free soul, and that is beautiful, but you also need to learn how to be an active participant in this earthly reality.

♃ ♑ | JUPITER IN CAPRICORN OR TENTH HOUSE

GIFT dedicated ambition

Jupiter in Capricorn is highly ambitious and will never back down. If you have a goal, there is no way you are not going to find a way to achieve it. You are extremely motivated and will make it your life's mission to figure out how to take your dreams and turn them into tangible realities. In fact, that is part of your gift and talent in this life. While others may dream of doing things, you have your dream and then set your mind to figuring out how to achieve it and help others achieve theirs too.

It's not good enough for you to climb to the top of the mountain. You want to climb it, build a restaurant on top, and then lay a pathway for others to go there. You want to see your dreams come to life right before your eyes. You want to be able to hold them in your hand and have your name on them so everyone can see it for years and generations to come.

Building a legacy is important to you, but remember this: your legacy is not in how many buildings have your name on it or how many goals you achieve; it is in how you treat others and how you show up for the ones you love. Your legacy is built in the small actions you take every single day. Success and ambition are all huge motivators and drivers for you in this life. Just keep in mind that this journey can have a price to pay if you lose sight of everything and everyone else in the process.

♃ ♒ | JUPITER IN AQUARIUS OR ELEVENTH HOUSE

GIFT seeing the bigger picture

Jupiter in Aquarius is full of light and hope for all of humanity and the state of the world. You are a humanitarian at heart and are always thinking of ways to make this world a better and safer place. While many are on a journey of self-discovery in this life, you are on a journey of figuring out how you can best help and support others. It is through your generosity and your expansive vision for the world that you are able to also grow in richness for yourself.

You have big dreams and you are going to need support to bring them to light. You are going to have to learn to work with others and share your unique vision and message—your dreams are so big, there is no way you can do it alone! You are all about bringing people together and creating community, so this should be something that comes naturally and easily to you. Using your generous heart to give and help others can bring great luck and fortune. The community and connections you build in this life are like family to you and, in turn, they are all like family to each other. You make life richer and more rewarding for those around you. Life is made for sharing, and you are leading the way.

♃ ♓ | JUPITER IN PISCES OR TWELFTH HOUSE

GIFT paving your own way

Getting lost in the thoughts of your mind and in the many options that life has to offer can make you feel like you are drifting out to sea without a life vest or a comfortable boat to sit in. At certain times of your life, it will feel this way, but this is all part of the experience.

Life has so much to offer you, and you are here to taste a little bit of it all. Don't feel like you have to choose just one path in this life or follow the tried-and-true way that society tells you is right. Everyone is on their own journey and everyone has their own path to pave. Being at sea is about learning to ride the waves of life. Sometimes they will be calm and other times they will be choppy, but they all create different skill sets and offer different opportunities.

Even though our soul comes into this life with a certain "programming" and a destiny to move through, it would defeat the purpose if we were given access to the ins and outs of what this may be. Learning to embrace this as the plan of your life can actually give you more direction and can help you feel grounded as you move through your life. Your lessons and gifts in this life are learning to surrender, go with the flow, and trust that your skills are always sharpening when you reach the roughest seas.

♃

10

Saturn

ZODIAC RULER Capricorn
KEYWORDS discipline, responsibility,
authority, dedication
RULES OVER relationship with father/masculine,
maturity, big business, government,
authority figures, laws, rules, boundaries

Saturn is like a strict teacher and is one of the most profound gateway planets on the journey to deeper truth, knowledge, and awareness. Saturn can bring hard lessons, but it is through those lessons that we can grow and achieve the most self-discovery. Just like that strict teacher, whenever we hand in our homework on time and excel in our tests, we get rewarded—the only difference is that these tests and lessons can't be learned through a textbook!

SATURN: LORD OF KARMA

Saturn is considered the Lord of Karma, because these hard lessons that greet us as we progress on our life journey are etched into our soul and are very much part of our destiny. It is through navigating the challenges Saturn brings that we can mature and transcend our past karma and reach higher states of enlightenment. Saturn can bring challenges—and gifts too.

Navigating the lessons of the Lord of Karma is something we do over the course of our lifetime. We can more closely track what these lessons may be by tracking the cycle of Saturn. Saturn spends about 2.5 years in each zodiac sign, and every 28.5 years it makes it back to the spot it was in at the time of your birth. This is known as your Saturn Return and is a very crucial time in astrology. Leading up to your Saturn Return and after your Saturn Return you will also experience a Saturn Opposition. Decoding this Saturn Cycle can help you dive deeper into whatever themes and messages the Lord of Karma is offering.

BORN WITH SATURN IN RETROGRADE?

♄℞ Saturn spends at least six months of the year in retrograde. Being born with Saturn in retrograde indicates that most of your growth in this life is on an internal level, rather than on an external one.

YOUR SATURN CYCLE

Saturn at birth: The sign and house of your Saturn at birth indicates your karmic destiny and what lessons, challenges, and growth you are set to achieve, especially on a soul level.

Saturn Square Saturn (age 7): You are learning the difference between right and wrong, and discovering consequences of your actions. You may be pushing the boundaries or learning how to navigate boundaries, which are now more apparent in your daily routine. You may lose your natural sensitivity to the spirit world and intuition, in favor of your five senses. You are still using imaginative play, but you are becoming more aware of your three-dimensional reality and the norms of society.

Saturn Opposite Saturn (age 14): This is a pivotal point when you are starting to see yourself as an individual, separate from your family and even friends. You may have dreams and ambitions that are different from the ideas and beliefs of your family, or you may challenge and test boundaries. On a deeper level, you are learning to feel comfortable in your own skin and to navigate what it means to be you.

Saturn Square Saturn (age 21): This is the final stage before your Saturn Return. You are learning to take responsibility for your life and what you want to achieve. On a deeper level, you are breaking free from your childhood conditioning and paving your own way.

Saturn Return (age 27 to 30): This is considered a cosmic rite of passage. You have completed your first Saturn Cycle and are now in a new stage of cosmic maturity. You have been through your first round of karmic lessons and you have made it!

During your Saturn Return, you may make big changes or realign your goals and values. You may have a new understanding of, or a new appreciation for, who you are and the journey you wish to travel. It's like the lessons you have been taking finally make sense and you can see with new eyes. You may feel restricted by things you thought you wanted, or you may feel a sense of needing to put your roots down and commit to something, whether it be a job, house, or relationship.

Saturn is the strict teacher, so we may feel challenged to reach new levels of personal growth, courage, and compassion. We are getting clearer about what we want and who we are, and it is no longer acceptable for these things to be ignored. We are growing up, and part of this process is paving our own way and doing things on our own terms.

This period can also bring an increased awareness of the boundaries of our lives. We may feel called to create more boundaries with people or with our family or jobs, or we may be called to pull down boundaries that have kept us closed off or hidden away. This is an empowering time, and it is usually not until this transit is over that we can make sense of it all. For most, the Saturn Return is well and truly completed by age thirty-one, and a new Saturn Cycle will begin again.

YOUR SATURN RETURN

· · · · · · · · ·

Think back to this age and reflect on what commitments you made or what boundaries you decided to push past. What lessons are you grateful for from this time? Or if you haven't reached this age yet, ask those around you what was happening in their life. What did they commit to more deeply? What did they decide to break free from? What karmic lessons and maturity did they go through during this time? You are likely to find themes that fit perfectly with Saturn Return.

After your first Saturn Return, you move on to start another Saturn Cycle. It is similar, but carries some different themes.

Saturn Opposition (age 42): You are advancing whatever gifts and lessons occurred during your Saturn Return. Have you fallen back into old habits, or are you taking the lessons being presented to you and running with them?

Second Saturn Return (age 58 to 60): While your first Saturn Return can bring challenges, your second Saturn Return is about stepping into a newfound wisdom. This is a time to embrace who you are and take responsibility for what you desire. You are setting new boundaries and figuring out what you are no longer willing to tolerate. You may search for new meaning or seek experiences that are enriching for your soul. You may gain a new sense of what is important to you, what you wish to spend your time doing, and whom you wish to spend your time with. This is a time of coming into your true self. It is about honoring your decisions, making peace with them, and moving forward with a greater sense of freedom and understanding. You are now beginning your third and final Saturn Cycle.

Saturn Opposition (age 73): Although you are on a new cycle, your last Saturn Return experience is being cemented. This is a humbling time when you may feel this sense that you have more years behind you than in front of you. You may feel a new passion for life and new experiences, or you may start thinking about your legacy.

Final Saturn Return (age 89): You have reached the third and final Saturn Cycle. You are able to look back with a greater sense of understanding and wisdom. There is a greater appreciation and gratitude for the small things, and life is lived in the present.

The sign and house your Saturn is in will color how you experience your Saturn Return and what themes are present.

♄♈ | SATURN IN ARIES OR FIRST HOUSE

KARMIC LESSON expanding and deepening how you define yourself

Your strength and power come when you are able to take the reins and lead the pack. You are a pioneer, and part of your purpose in this life is to create something new and bring bold new innovations to the planet. By expressing your unique essence, you are able to shine your light and lift and inspire others. Part of your karma in this life is in learning how to tame your inner fire and stand up for yourself, while also taking into consideration those around you.

How can you assert yourself and express your individuality in a healthy way? Your lesson is in learning to do this, but also in learning how to work with others and maintain healthy relationships. While you are a pioneer and a leader, you need the support of those around you. Follow your vision and set your boundaries, but also be mindful not to push people away in the process.

You may have the tendency to run or want to retreat when things get challenging or uncomfortable. Over the years, learning to stay and navigate through these challenges, rather than run from them, can help you achieve the most growth and reward.

♄♉ | SATURN IN TAURUS OR SECOND HOUSE

KARMIC LESSON knowing your true self-worth and what you value

You are extremely hardworking and tend to view life as a challenge that needs to be overcome. You may feel concerned with safety and create boundaries that give you a sense of stability and routine. While there is nothing wrong with this, be mindful of boxing yourself in too much. Sometimes there can be great rewards and opportunities when you take risks and learn to leave the safety and comfort of what you have always known.

While you like to take a methodical and measured approach to everything you do, sometimes you also have to trust your heart and believe that things will always work out how and when they are supposed to. Finding a way to feel secure and confident in yourself will help with this process and will allow you to feel brave enough to take those risks and break free of self-imposed boundaries. You hold yourself back; sometimes that is necessary, but often it is limiting the potential you can achieve in this life.

Part of your karmic lessons in this life also revolve around where you choose to spend your energy. This includes how you choose to spend your time, whom you choose to spend your time with, and how you also choose to spend your money. Getting clear on your values will help with this, and will allow you to know whether you are spending your energy on things that matter or things that are simply a distraction from your higher truth.

♄♊ | SATURN IN GEMINI OR THIRD HOUSE

KARMIC LESSON speaking your truth and using your voice

Part of your karmic lessons in this life revolve around communication. In this life, your words, or lack of words, can get you into trouble at times. You can find yourself in strife when you share too much. Just the same, you can also face challenges when you hold back and censor your true thoughts and feelings. Mindful communication is an extremely difficult skill to master, but in this life, it is an important one for you. As you navigate through your life, you will eventually develop the skills you need, and you may discover the power that your words and your silence can have.

As you master your ability to communicate, you are going to have to also be mindful to not use your skills to manipulate or con others into getting your own way. When you do, strict teacher Saturn can bring some hard knocks, forcing you to get into line. Your purpose in this life is to take responsibility for the words that you speak and the motives behind them. When your motives are aligned with your true self, you are going to find that they are able to open doors for you and bring exciting opportunities. We all grow from challenges: part of this experience in life is making mistakes, or taking risks that sometimes don't work out. Keep checking in with yourself and ensure that your morals and values are aligned with where you want them to be.

♄♋ | SATURN IN CANCER OR FOURTH HOUSE

KARMIC LESSON creating boundaries even with those you love

Part of your karmic lessons in this life stems from your upbringing and the relationship that you have with your family. Before you came into this body, you existed as an eternal soul in another realm. As this eternal soul, you decided the lessons and journey you wanted to experience in this life and chose the family that would be the perfect fit for you. You chose your family based not on how amazing they would be, but how much they would support your soul journey and the things that you wanted to learn in this life.

While this is true for all souls, having Saturn in Cancer indicates an emphasis when it comes to family karma. You chose your family for your own growth and development, and to inspire the breaking of generational patterns that are no longer serving. While you may feel weighted and held down by your family at times, learning to tune in to the powerful love that you are will allow you to break free from this and assert a new level of independence.

Part of your journey is learning to break out of family patterns and cycles that don't align with you and to show that a new and better way can be achieved. Learning to love yourself is a key to finding the strength and the confidence to break the generational cycles that are playing out. Another way to look at this is ending the emotional traumas that are carried through your generational bloodline. For example, if your mother was abused and had not worked through this abuse, her trauma may have influenced the way she raised you. If you don't ever address this, then the cycle carries on in the way you choose to raise your own children or even in your personal relationships, and so on. This is what you have come to break and transcend in this life. It may not be as obvious as this, but it's important to learn to shift the behaviors and patterns of how you were raised so you can create healthier and more loving relationships.

♄♌ | SATURN IN LEO OR FIFTH HOUSE

KARMIC LESSON putting yourself and your ideas out there

Part of your karmic lessons is learning to navigate the abundance that is always around you. Most of us think of abundance as money and having plenty of things surrounding us: a big car, a fancy house, and so on. But abundance is about tuning in to the energy of what is on offer. Like the endless blue sky or the grains of sand on the beach, abundance is seeing the opportunities that are always unfolding, just the same way a flower blooms or the trees grow back their leaves in the spring.

Abundance is all around us and comes in many different forms. For you, learning to appreciate the abundance in all things and in all states of your life is what the journey is all about. You may experience challenges with money—you could have too much or too little. Or you may find yourself working your way from the bottom to the top, or the top to the bottom. Chasing status, luxury, and riches can sound like a good idea, and life is geared for us to do this, but it is not going to serve you in this life.

You may feel blinded by the bright lights of riches and fame throughout your life, but know that true happiness and fulfillment is an inside job. It is learning to see the bigger picture and to understand that all jobs are important and all people are important. Everyone is here because they have something to give, and their light and spark of energy is just as important as the next person's. We are all in this together, so an important part of your life journey is to find respect for yourself no matter how "successful" you deem yourself to be, and to have respect for others, no matter how successful you deem them to be.

♄♍ | SATURN IN VIRGO OR SIXTH HOUSE

KARMIC LESSON creating healthy habits

You have great discipline and strive for perfection in everything you do. You like to follow the rules and do things to the letter. You like to follow the instructions, but sometimes in life, not everything comes with instructions to follow. It is moments like these when you do your most growth work. While growth can be challenging, when you have only your inner wisdom to rely on, that is when you make some of the bravest, boldest, and most successful leaps of your life.

Following the guidebooks is great, but there is something empowering about putting them away and following your inner guide. Connect with your inner voice and your intuition and follow that guidance instead. You always know the way, and you always know what is best. Learn to trust yourself and that powerhouse of wisdom and knowledge that you have come into this life with.

When you connect with your soul through practices such as meditation, healing work, and the like, you can step into a new, independent power that can help you take the instructions and work of others and add your own unique flair and spin. Saturn is the strict teacher, but its aim is to not make you the same; it wants to make you better. It wants the student to become the master, and this is part of your karmic lessons in this life. You are here to become a master by learning through others, but more importantly, by learning through trusting yourself.

♄♎ | SATURN IN LIBRA OR SEVENTH HOUSE

KARMIC LESSON building healthy relationships

Many of your karmic lessons in this life revolve around your relationships and the people you encounter on your journey. It is like each one of them is a teacher, imparting wisdom and knowledge and moving on when the lesson is done. Your relationships are likely to be a big theme, for you are on a journey of learning to hold your own space, even while in the presence of others. You are learning to stand up for yourself and set your boundaries, so you are not losing yourself in the thoughts and feelings of others. But you are also learning how to connect and create deeper and more loving relationships in the process. Essentially, as you learn to stand in your own truth and in your own energy, without being sidetracked by others, you create more meaningful and loving relationships.

On a spiritual level, life may also highlight to you how those around you can be a mirror for your own triggers and what is happening within you. When we meet a challenging person, it is easy to get annoyed by them and judge them. But it can sometimes be more rewarding to think about what parts of ourselves are getting triggered and why that may be. When we judge another, we are judging ourselves, so stopping to look at this can help bring some clarity or deeper awareness into why we feel the way we do. Releasing these judgments and replacing them with the idea that everyone is doing the best they can from their level of awareness can create more compassion.

Setting boundaries with others is also important, but you don't want these boundaries to box you in either. Work on creating boundaries by standing up for yourself, staying true to yourself, but also learning how to love, even if it has to be from a distance.

♄♏ | SATURN IN SCORPIO OR EIGHTH HOUSE

KARMIC LESSON *trusting your inner knowing*

Part of your karmic lessons in this life is learning how to keep evolving and embracing the changes that come your way as you move through your life. Change can be scary, but you are here to learn how to embrace change and to work through the transformations that take place when you are brave enough to make a change. We all get comfortable staying in our safe spaces, but your job in this life is to identify when you have outgrown your safe space and to get to work on taking the next step into the new. Fear can be a debilitating presence. In this life, you are working through your fear of change and your fear of things transitioning and moving forward.

Nothing is ever lost, and nature can teach us that. Although the leaves fall from the trees, they always return. And the same is true for life. Life is energy, and energy can never be created or destroyed. It just shifts from one form to another. Your life is always doing the same. Even though things may be removed or cleared from your life, there is always something new coming in to take its place. Trusting this process and allowing yourself to move through the changes and transitions that come your way can lead to a new power and can help you step into a more confident and aligned place.

You have a resilient soul, and you are able to handle the darker notes of life better than anyone else. Surrendering to the dark unknown that often comes along with change is where your creative powers lie. This is how you can keep reinventing yourself and moving to higher levels of awareness and consciousness. Life is meant to be experienced, so don't get stuck where you are. Acknowledge the fear, but also know that amazing things can happen when you take a leap of faith and allow your life to transform.

♄♐ | SATURN IN SAGITTARIUS OR NINTH HOUSE

KARMIC LESSON *expanding what you already know*

You want to run free with the wind, but life has other plans and responsibilities that crop up to hold you back. It can seem unfair, but in this life, part of your karmic journey is learning how to take responsibility for your choices and actions. You are being asked to take a slower and more methodical approach to your life, and to think carefully before acting. While there is a part of you that may want to race ahead, the more conservative and cautious side of you will get the last say.

There is something for you to learn in this more cautious approach to life. There is some wisdom in learning how to set boundaries and follow the rules. Eventually, this way of living can get a little, well, boring. If you don't give your desire for freedom an outlet, you are going to encounter this boredom and perhaps also feel angry or disgruntled with the direction of your life. Yes, you have responsibilities that need attending to that are difficult to escape, but you also have to make the time to focus on joy and play.

Sagittarius is represented by the arrow of the archer. The arrow is your responsibility to figure out in which direction you are going to aim it. Where you aim it has consequences. But once you make your mark and release your arrow, that is where you can allow things to unravel with a little more freedom and trust. Your arrow becomes your focus, but you can enjoy the journey and the freedom to reach your destination and retrieve your arrow in your own time.

There is a bright spark of optimism in you. Don't let it flicker away because you feel the heavy weight of responsibility creeping in. There is a power and a strength in learning to step up and take charge of your life. There is a strength that comes when you choose to own your life and the journey you are taking. Reclaim that spark by honoring the balance between the direction of your arrow and the free blowing wind that gets to carry it.

♄♑ | SATURN IN CAPRICORN OR TENTH HOUSE

KARMIC LESSON redefining success

Saturn is ruled by Capricorn, so you embody the purest expression of its energy. You are logical and hardworking, and driven by your ambitions. Through the first part of your life you may crave discipline and flourish when you are given clear guidance and boundaries. You may also find that your true power and potential are able to come through when you are pushed and stretched to your limits. This isn't something that is sustainable; eventually you will have to find a balance between working hard and going for your ambitions, and also learning to lighten up and enjoy the unfolding of your life.

We are all climbing our own mountains in this life, but the aim is not to get to the top. The aim is to enjoy the process, no matter where our final destination may be. If you don't learn to embrace this, eventually you will find yourself feeling burnt out, or playing out your ambitions and drive for success with the relationships in your life. Not everyone shares your hardworking approach or ambitious drive. Pushing this on others or requiring others to do the same may lead to resentment instead.

Your karmic lesson in this life is learning not to work harder but to work smarter. Your journey is about taking these ambitions and fighting for them, but not at the expense of your well-being or the well-being of others. It is all very well to be successful in this life, but if you are miserable when you get there, if you have trodden on toes and abandoned your family in the process, was it all worth it?

Your lesson in this life is learning to enjoy the process. Set your sights not on your destination but in each and every moment that has been given to you. Learn to balance your energy levels and not burn yourself out chasing success. You need to give yourself boundaries when it comes to your work ethic, your ambitions, and your definition of success. You also need to learn to not be so hard on yourself and others, and to embrace the softer and gentler sides of your personality. Goals and ambitions are far more rewarding when they spark joy.

♄ ♒ | SATURN IN AQUARIUS OR ELEVENTH HOUSE

KARMIC LESSON listening to your own needs

Part of your karmic lessons in this life is learning to separate yourself from those around you. You can become too wrapped up in the energies of others or too concerned with what others are doing, and that causes you to lose sight of your own way. In relationships, you may find that you give too much of yourself away, or you find it difficult to set boundaries that allow the relationship to progress in a healthy way. You have an all-or-nothing approach, and often this approach can lead you in circles.

Part of your karmic lesson in this life is learning to find your true center and maintain your independence in your relationships. Rather than rely on those around you, you need to learn to rely on yourself and find a way to be self-sufficient, even when you are in a committed relationship. Those you encounter in this life are powerful teachers for you and may challenge you to embrace this more independent way of being.

Saturn in Aquarius also indicates that part of your purpose is to bring a higher vision to the world. You have a big heart, and while this can land you in codependent relationships, it can also inspire a new way of doing things and a new way to think about how humanity can best be served. Your big heart coupled with your great organizational skills can see you do a lot of good in your community and for the world at large. You can be an angel for others and have the power and potential to bring more love, healing, and support to the world.

KARMIC LESSON balancing discipline and creativity

Don't shy away from your creative inspirations and ideas. You may feel the need to protect and hide yourself away, but when you allow your light to shine, there is a creative potential that can be unlocked. Your creative innovations and designs are a gift to this world, so don't hold yourself back from sharing your creativity, in whatever form it comes to you.

Part of your karmic lessons in this life is learning to take this incredible creativity that you have and bring some discipline or grounded energy to it. While the act of creativity requires us to release groundedness and embrace a sense of freedom, you are called to leave your feet on the ground but to let the rest of you wander. This is how you can do your best creative work and still find a sense of discipline in bringing your creative ideas into tangible reality. Without staying grounded, your creative ideas are only ideas. It is getting grounded that allows you to turn your creativity into tangible projects that can inspire and be shared by others.

Along with your amazing creative talents, you are also deeply spiritual and may feel that you have walked this Earth many times before. You may feel like you are an old soul, or perhaps people comment that you are wise beyond your years. You have a deep wisdom inside of you and an innate understanding of spirituality. Just like your creativity, having a grounded spiritual practice can help you create a sense of balance and dive deeper into your inner knowing. You are in the physical world, so don't get lost in your mind or in the spirit realms. You are a soul with a physical body for a reason, and it is up to you to embrace and find that reason.

CHIRON

Nestled between Saturn and Uranus is the asteroid Chiron, which is known in astrology as the wounded healer. Chiron is also referred to as the rainbow bridge, as it links the gateway planets to the planets of higher consciousness. When we explore Uranus, Neptune, and Pluto, we will see that their energy is much more spiritual and less tangible, and their energies flow on more of a subconscious level. It is this bridge between the more physical "real world" and the spirit world that Chiron helps balance.

In our natal astrology chart, Chiron represents the wounds we have come into this life to work through and transcend. These wounds are not meant to be portals of weakness but portals of strength. When we are able to understand and nurture our wounds, they become our source of healing and power. As the poet Rumi says, "The wound is the place where the Light enters you" and that is Chiron's message. Our wounds make us more human and more compassionate. They remind us that as we heal and work through our wounds, we are helping ourselves and the generations that follow.

Planets of Higher Consciousness

URANUS   NEPTUNE   PLUTO

The planets of higher consciousness are Uranus, Neptune, and Pluto. These planets work with us on a subconscious level, which means we don't notice their lessons and gifts unless we are paying attention. As these planets work quietly in the background of our lives, it is often only once they are done that we are able to see the journey of transformation we have gone through. As these planets take years to orbit the Sun, their effects can also be seen on a global or generational level.

11

Uranus

ZODIAC RULER Aquarius
KEYWORDS innovation, surprise, change,
upheaval, rebellion, freedom
RULES OVER science, futuristic technology,
artificial intelligence, humanitarianism, natural disasters,
astrology, kundalini/spiritual awakenings.

Has anything ever happened to you that took you by complete surprise and radically changed and shifted your whole world overnight? That was likely the work of Uranus. Uranus is known as the great awakener for its energy that brings radical change—the change that causes revolution and upheaval to pave the way for a brighter future. Uranus awakens us to a new truth and a new power by breaking us free from the things that are no longer serving us and the things that no longer support our highest growth.

URANUS: THE GREAT AWAKENER

Uranus is unstable, unreliable, and surprising, but that's the way it needs to be—that is how it gets us to open our eyes and awaken to what needs to shift. All those moments when life has caught you off guard, or something has come out of the blue and totally rocked and changed your world, that is Uranus in action.

Uranus's energy can stir the winds of change. It can make things rattle and shake, but when the pieces land, we are left with a new truth and a new way of seeing things. Uranus wants us to change and keep evolving, and the only way it can do this is by shaking things up every now and again to show us there is a different and better way to live and be.

Uranus also represents modern innovation, entrepreneurship, and forward thinking. Uranus is the radical, the revolutionary that is always pushing boundaries and helping us get out of our comfort zone. Uranus wants to break down walls and remove boundaries. It wants us to find our freedom from labels and from judgments, and to see each other as one. Uranus also rules the advancement of technology. Its energy inspires us to keep dreaming up inventive ways that technology can change the world and integrate into our lives.

URANUS CYCLE

Uranus takes about eighty-four years to orbit the Sun. This means it takes eighty-four years to return to the spot it was in at the time of your birth and complete a full cycle. Here's how you can track your Uranus Cycle.

Uranus Square (age 20 to 22): We feel called to find our freedom and individuality. We want to break free from what we have learned in school or in the home so we can pave our own way. We may find ourselves in intense relationships or seeking intense experiences to challenge what we know about ourselves.

Uranus Opposition (age 40 to 44): This is known as the "midlife crisis." We feel a desire to rebel against or question the life we have chosen or the restrictions and limitations we may be feeling within the home, family life, or work. We may feel we are destined for more, or that we want to pursue dreams we had forgotten about or put by the wayside. This is a powerful time for stepping into a new truth and authenticity. Our true colors are likely to be revealed, and we may want to own more of who we are. We may also take greater risks or make decisions we would have been afraid to make. Chaos can unfold, but this only helps us to see what is meant for us and what has to fall away. The best way to navigate through any challenges is to go with the flow and to release control. Uranus is about surrendering and allowing the pieces to fall where they may. If we let them fall, they will point and guide us to the answers we are seeking.

URANUS AND KUNDALINI AWAKENINGS

....

Uranus rules over *kundalini* energy. Kundalini is a Sanskrit term that means "coiled one," which refers to the life force energy that lives within each of us. We can picture this as a coiled snake that lives at the base of our spine until it is triggered to awaken. The awakening and uncoiling of the snake allows this powerful energy to rise up our spine, activating and awakening our energy centers, intuition, and connection to the divine.

Kundalini energy can be felt as electricity or tingles moving through the body, and can bring spiritual awakenings and realizations that guide us to a more spiritual path. The shocks and surprises that Uranus can bring can activate this coiled snake within us. Uranus can help shake and awaken our life force energy, reconnecting us with our higher truth.

Uranus Square (age 60 to 62): We feel a call to step into a new power and to claim our freedom. We may feel a desire to change our way of life and to let go of the things we once feared. This is a powerful time when we can learn to love and own all of who we are and the decisions we have made. Whether we label them as bad or good, they have made us the person we are today.

Uranus Return (age 84): The Uranus Cycle has been completed. If we are lucky enough to experience this, we may reach a new level of freedom. Our bodies may have slowed, but from within, we can find peace, acceptance, and a surrendering to our life. We may live more in the moment and learn how to release total and complete control so we can enjoy whatever opportunities and experiences life continues to bring our way.

While Uranus is always helping us find a new level of freedom, it often does this by bringing shocking and surprising events our way that are emotionally charged. While this can be challenging, we also have the opportunity to choose to see them as powerful portals of awakening that can guide us deeper into an understanding of our soul's path and purpose.

The sign that Uranus was in at the time of your birth can indicate where you long to feel freedom and what changes or revolutions your soul is destined to bring to the planet. Because Uranus spends over seven years in each sign, the sign that it is in can indicate the energy you are working with and what your generation has come to shift and change.

While learning about the sign that Uranus was in at the time of your birth is helpful, you can also tune in to the energy of Uranus as it makes its way through each zodiac sign.

♅♈ | URANUS IN ARIES OR FIRST HOUSE

GENERATIONAL LESSON to break the status quo and long-standing
traditions and find new ways of doing things

You are a headstrong, passionate, and fiery soul that has come here to pave a new path forward, one that has never been done before. While your mind is full of ingenious ideas, you may also get carried away and be unable to focus on the task at hand. You may have plenty of ideas, but lack the groundedness and the focus to actually execute them.

Your fiery nature can also be your own worst enemy. It can help drive your purpose and your passions, but it can also cause your temper to flare and make you hold on to resentments and betrayal. Keeping these things close to your heart will never serve you, so rather than plotting an elaborate way to get revenge, it is better to release it, bring acceptance to it, and work on forgiveness. If you get caught up in your head or stuck in the past, imagine your energy moving out of your head, down your feet, and into the earth, where it can be cleansed. Simply visualize this in your mind and allow yourself to feel the lightness that follows.

Uranus was last in Aries from 2010 through 2019. Think about how you found a new sense of independence or took a risk to go after your dreams and goals.

♅♉ | URANUS IN TAURUS OR SECOND HOUSE

GENERATIONAL LESSON to focus on healing the planet
and looking after the resources we have been given

You are a builder, and part of your purpose in this life is to take your creative and inventive ideas and turn them into realities. While others may daydream about changing the world, you are able to take the daydream and create a plan of actionable steps. You have the gift of taking creative ideas and inspirations and bringing them to life in a real and tangible way.

While this steady and methodical approach helps you make leaps and bounds, it is also important that you allow yourself to be flexible and adaptable to any road bumps that may greet you along the way. Changing your plans or routine does not sit well with you, but a powerful lesson is learning to embrace the ups and downs of life and flow with the winds of change when they blow in your direction. When you get stuck in one area of your life for too long, or too fixated on your plans, it's most likely a sign that the time has come to pivot or let go. Acknowledge what holds you back or what you are clinging to, and then allow yourself to break free so you can move forward. While you crave stability, no growth can come from remaining in your comfort zone forever.

At the time of writing this book, Uranus is touring through the sign of Taurus, and we all have the power to tune in to this energy. Taurus typically does not like change, so with Uranus (the planet of change) in this sign, you may feel a push-pull between making changes and holding on to what's tried and true. Uranus in Taurus can also shine a spotlight on the environment and how you choose to use the Earth's resources. Uranus will be in Taurus from 2018 through 2026 and won't return again to this placement for another eighty-four years.

URANUS DATES

The dates for Uranus through the signs may overlap due to its retrograde movements.

♅♊ | URANUS IN GEMINI OR THIRD HOUSE

GENERATIONAL LESSON to keep an open mind and
to bring people together using technology

You are highly perceptive, and your mind is like a sponge, soaking up things from the world around you. You have sharp intuition and a knack for picking up on subtle clues in your environment and in people you have only just met. All of this makes you highly attractive and charming, and perhaps people feel like they know you after just having met you. While you have this amazing ability, you can also morph and adapt to whatever situation you find yourself in. This ability to adapt can come in handy in a variety of social situations, but it can also be used to manipulate and take advantage of others. Be mindful if you find yourself doing this, and know you don't always need to have the upper hand. By keeping your ego in check, you can use this incredible energy to network and create special and lifelong bonds with those who cross your path.

You are a student of life, and everyone you meet has some wisdom to impart. Keep an open mind and always be open to learning new things; when you do, you will find that you can thrive. It is often through the connections you build and the relationships you create that you can find your way to your path and purpose.

Uranus enters Gemini from 2026 through 2033. We are likely to see new innovations when it comes to communication and how we connect with one another.

♅

GENERATIONAL LESSON to bring change to family dynamics
and the way people choose to live

There is this deeper longing to feel like you belong, but the harder you try to fit in, the more alone you feel. When you embrace your true authenticity, when you own all of who you are, you will naturally attract a supportive and loving environment around you.

Part of your purpose in this life is learning how to radically accept yourself and your past, and then to take that radical acceptance and use it to shine your light and go for your goals. Wholeheartedly accepting who you are allows you to feel strong and confident to go after what you want, and to bring your creative ideas and visions to the table. Be mindful of when you find yourself playing small or when you shrink back to fit in or be agreeable. You are your strongest when you can own all of who you are, so keep showing up in your truth.

Keep shining your light and moving from your heart. You have a strong heart energy field, so tune in to the wisdom of your heart when you are feeling stuck. Place your hand over your heart and listen to its direction and guidance.

While part of your purpose is to find a sense of belonging in whatever circumstances life brings your way, know that it is also okay to retreat into your shell when you feel the need. With a sensitive heart, you need to give yourself time to recharge your batteries and ground yourself before heading back into the world with your heart on your sleeve.

Uranus was last in Cancer from 1948 through 1956. This period was the start of the baby boomer years, which brought many changes to home and family life—both being ruled by Cancer. Uranus will enter Cancer again from 2033 through 2040 and maybe during this period, we may again see radical shifts and changes to home and family life.

♅♌ | URANUS IN LEO OR FIFTH HOUSE

GENERATIONAL LESSON to bring change to how we choose to lead and guide people

You have bold ideas and a clear vision for how you can create a brighter future. When you feel passionate about something, when you follow the beat of your heart, there is little you cannot achieve. However, you need to be mindful of allowing your pride and ego to get in the way. While you have the gift of coming up with innovative and forward-thinking ideas, you need to learn to work as a team and collaborate with your efforts rather than dominate.

Part of your purpose in this life is stepping into your role as a leader. To be a good leader, you have to aim toward unity and understanding, rather than trying to tell people what to do. Watch for where you may be doing this in your own life and ask yourself, "Is there a better and more balanced way to handle it?" By releasing control and working with people, you naturally step into your true leadership potential. Along with being a natural-born leader, you are also highly creative, and when you tune in and connect with this creativity, you will always be able to find solutions to your problems.

Uranus was last in Leo from 1955 through 1962. During this time, people felt more comfortable expressing their creativity, and different styles of music including rock 'n roll hit the scene. Uranus won't enter Leo again until 2040, and during this seven-year period, we are likely to see changes to the entertainment and creative industries, as well as shifts when it comes to leadership. Leo also rules over royalty, so we may also see significant shifts when it comes to royal families around the world.

♅ ♍ | URANUS IN VIRGO OR SIXTH HOUSE

GENERATIONAL LESSON to find our strength and independence

You have the mind of a seeker and are always looking for new experiences. While you love trying new things, your aim is often to perfect things or to perfect life. You want to try it all before settling on your decision. While this can sometimes be a smart approach to making decisions, it can also slow you down and get you stuck in your head, for every experience you try has something to offer and something to consider.

Part of your purpose in this life is learning how to get out of your head and into the spontaneity of your heart. Sometimes you will not have access to all the information needed to make the best and most perfect decision, and that is okay. It is okay to make a mistake. It is okay to try, realize something is not for you, and try again. Your intuition can also be a powerful source of wisdom, especially when the facts are not as clear as you would like them to be. The more you trust yourself and your intuition, the easier it will be for you to make those decisions when you find yourself at a fork in the road.

Along with trusting your intuition, claiming your independence is also a source of power. While it is fine to rely on others, in this life, you need to develop your own independence and inner strength. You need to tune in to that part of you that may not always have the answers, but has the strength and the determination to make it through no matter what life brings your way. You are a pioneer when it comes to showing people the power that can be found when they tune in to their inner strength and find their sense of independence and freedom.

Uranus was last in Virgo from 1961 through 1969. During this time, there were many innovations when it came to medicine and health care thanks to improvements in technology. Health care is typically ruled by Virgo and technology is ruled by Uranus, so when we see this combination again in 2045, we are likely to experience advancements in these areas.

♅♎ | URANUS IN LIBRA OR SEVENTH HOUSE

You are here to explore and grow through the people you surround yourself with. You may find yourself drawn to an eclectic group of people, or you may find you love to surround yourself with people who are different from you in order to grow and learn. Having a sense of freedom is important to you, especially when it comes to the person you choose to partner with. You may also long for creative freedom in the workplace, and you may struggle when you are given too rigid of an approach. You have the natural gift of seeing things from a balanced and fair state of mind. You can shift yourself out of the confusion of the now and see things from a bird's-eye perspective to create a more holistic viewpoint. This ability can make you empathetic, and you are a person many people trust or feel safe confiding in.

While you do long for freedom, you are extremely loyal and can often tell when someone is lying or trying to deceive you. In fact, you are a good judge of character and have a strong intuition when someone or something is not right. As you learn to listen and strengthen your intuition, you may find you can pick up on subtle energies and clues from the world around you.

You may also feel yourself absorbing or taking on the emotions of others. If this ever gets overwhelming, be sure to come back to your center and work on grounding yourself and your energy. You can do this by walking barefoot on the grass or taking a few deep belly breaths. As you move through your soul journey, you are likely to have a positive and even life-changing effect on those around you.

Uranus was last in Libra from 1968 through 1975. During this time, there was a significant increase in the number of divorces. The shame around divorce subsided and more people were looking for freedom in their relationships. When Uranus enters Libra again in the 2050s, we are also likely to see changes to marriage and relationships, and perhaps also the justice system.

♅♏ | URANUS IN SCORPIO OR EIGHTH HOUSE

You are always seeking to understand yourself better and the deeper meaning behind what you are feeling or experiencing. When you learn to go within and unpack your traumas or those uncomfortable emotions, a great breakthrough can occur.

Part of your purpose in this life is learning to take a journey of self-inquiry and to keep doing the work to understand yourself on a deeper level. Through this understanding, you can unlock new potentials and push yourself further in life. It's almost like you came into this world with some jewels of wisdom buried within you. As you seek to understand yourself and your upbringing, you can use these jewels of wisdom to transform yourself and your life for the better. Know as you go within and bring a sense of acceptance to who you are that you can make leaps and bounds in this life and attract more of what you desire.

Uranus was last in Scorpio in 1974 through 1981. During this time, there was a deep dive into psychology and understanding of mental illnesses. Going to therapy became more mainstream, and there was also a greater emergence of self-help literature. Uranus won't return to Scorpio again until 2058. At this time we may see developments when it comes to psychology and understanding our thoughts and emotions and how they impact us.

♅ ♐ | URANUS IN SAGITTARIUS OR NINTH HOUSE

GENERATIONAL LESSON to change how we view ourselves spiritually
and our higher purpose for living

You crave freedom when it comes to going after your purpose and doing what will fulfill you and make you happy. You are not content doing something for the sake of doing it; it has to have meaning for you. There has to be a bigger or greater why for you to be interested in pursuing something. When that bigger reason ceases to exist, you may leave years of work and dedication behind to seek something new. While those around you may recommend that you finish what you started, this is not a good enough reason for you. There has to be a purpose, and when that purpose has been lost or has changed, it is time to move on.

If you ever feel stagnant or stuck, look to your goals and what you are pursuing: Is the purpose still there? Are you still moving forward with your purpose and passion in the driver's seat? If not, it may be time for a change or to restructure a particular area of your life. Our dreams grow and change as we do, so it's important we keep updating them and not fear moving on to the next thing when the time is right.

You are a seeker of truth, but this seeking can get you into trouble because very often, everyone has their own version of the truth. While you may want people to see things your way, that is not always going to be the case, and there may be harsh lessons for you if you try to move through your life with this mindset. It is far more powerful for you to enter a place where you are free and brave enough to seek your personal truths and to be okay with the fact that they may not be other people's truths.

Uranus was last in Sagittarius from 1981 through 1988. During this time, there was a shift when it came to seeking the truth, especially on a spiritual level. Fewer people identified with being religious, and international travel became more accessible. As people traveled around the world, they learned new truths and developed a deeper understanding of humanity. Uranus will return to Sagittarius in 2065 and at this time we may see new understandings or changes in religion and spirituality and perhaps also travel.

♅ ♑ | URANUS IN CAPRICORN OR TENTH HOUSE

GENERATIONAL LESSON to overhaul and bring change
to traditional or "tried and true" establishments

The sky's the limit! You have a natural ability to take what has been tested and proven and add to it to make it better or make it your own.

Part of your purpose is walking the well-traveled road but finding new ways to approach it and new ways to think about it. You can bring innovation to long-standing traditions and create new meaning from them. In a sense, you can find this perfect balance between respecting and honoring traditions and making them more relevant to the world we live in today. When you use this approach, you can excel, especially with your career and in matters of business. You can take what has already been built and what has been laid before you and make it better. You have a natural authority and power, and when you use this in a productive way, you can easily win over respect and get things done.

Uranus was last in Capricorn from 1988 to 1996. At this time the Internet became more popular and more people had computers in their home. This opened the door for many traditional businesses to shift and innovate to keep up with emerging trends. The next time Uranus enters Capricorn will be in the 2070s and once again, we are likely to see shifts that will force traditional and long-standing businesses to innovate or be left behind.

♅ ♒ | URANUS IN AQUARIUS OR ELEVENTH HOUSE

GENERATIONAL LESSON to bring change and radical advancements to technology
and to take part in creating a society built on equality

Uranus is ruled by Aquarius, so you have its energy true and strong. Uranus is the bringer of change, and you thrive under change. You may even seek change to keep your life interesting. You are an innovator and may find you are naturally gifted and drawn to technology. You were born in the technology age, and your generation is destined to bring radical advancements and innovations when it comes to this arena.

You have an entrepreneurial soul, and you have the natural ability to find ways to do things in a more effective and automated manner. You crave freedom, like to make your own rules, and do things to the beat of your own drum. You may also feel driven to support humanitarian causes and to focus on building a world that is more fair, just, and equal. You are motivated when the things you are doing are supporting a good cause and are helping to create a better world and future not just for yourself, but for all humanity.

Uranus was last in Aquarius from 1995 through 2003, which was the height of the dot-com boom. Huge advancements in technology were seen at this time, and mobile phones became more commonplace. The next time Uranus enters its ruling sign of Aquarius is in the 2080s, when we are likely to see huge shifts and advancements in technology that take us into the next era.

♅♓ | URANUS IN PISCES OR TWELFTH HOUSE

GENERATIONAL LESSON to recognize the oneness in each other
and to hold the vision of creating a beautiful and better world

Uranus in Pisces is dreamy, creative, and loves nothing more than to escape from reality. This can be through movies, traveling, or getting lost in a good book. You may find yourself drawn to fantasy worlds or deep diving into your spiritual journey.

Having Uranus in Pisces indicates a strong creative vision, and it is part of your purpose in this life to share these creative visions and sparks with the world around you. The more you can shine in your true unique essence, the easier this will be. Being creative can be like an antidote, so give yourself permission to wander off and daydream every once in a while. Use these grand visions that come to you to inspire your work and give back to the world. In times of stress, you may also benefit from taking time to rest, recharge, and lose yourself in something that brings you joy and fills you up.

Uranus was last in Pisces from 2003 through 2010. During this time, we saw a rise in the New Age spiritual movement, and books about wizards, vampires, and other mythical and magical creatures became exceedingly popular. Uranus in Pisces is about escaping this physical earthly dimension and diving into other realms; we just have to remember to keep ourselves grounded as we allow our imaginations to soar.

12

Neptune

ZODIAC RULER Pisces
KEYWORDS illusions, dreams, confusion, creativity
RULES OVER dreams, intuition, visual arts/photography,
entertainment industry, movies, theater, magic,
alcohol/drugs/escapism

Neptune is the planet of dreams, illusions, and higher consciousness. It is creative, artistic, and loves to escape reality. Neptune is also believed to be a gateway to higher realms and the home of unconditional love. When its energy shines down on the planet and in our own lives, we are reminded that we are all connected and our souls are all from the same family. No matter our differences, Neptune reminds us that we are more similar than we realize and more connected than we will ever know.

NEPTUNE: THE PLANET OF DREAMS

On a surface level, Neptune's energy can feel foggy and confusing. It can feel like we are wading through a dark forest without a light to guide us. To proceed, we have to move forward carefully and slowly and to trust our other senses to guide us—especially our sixth sense.

Neptune encourages us to use our intuition and remember we are far wiser and more psychic than we have been made to believe. We all hold this potential within; it is just that most of us are never encouraged to use it or trust it.

Neptune asks us to trust ourselves. It calls for us to stop looking with our eyes all the time, and to see with the "eye." When we can transcend Neptune's lessons, we are able to push past the fogginess and shift into higher realms of consciousness and understanding. Suddenly, the fogginess is not there to bother us but to guide us to go within and to trust the unseen world rather than look for answers in the tangible world around us.

For most of us, our first encounter with strong Neptune energy is when transiting Neptune makes a square to your natal Neptune. This is called your Neptune Square and happens around the ages of 38 to 42.

Neptune Square (ages 38 to 42): You may feel the fog roll in and question what is real and what is not. Things you may have believed were true and real may dissolve, or ideas you had held may shatter like they were never real. This is a time when the road ahead doesn't seem clear or you feel you have lost your way and are unsure of what matters to you anymore.

At this stage in our lives, we question things more deeply to discover new truths. What is my truth? Who am I really? Our answers often come through spiritual reflection. If you are yet to walk a spiritual path or connect with your spirituality, you may feel called to do so. Alternatively, if you have been walking a spiritual path, you may be called to go deeper or to teach and share your wisdom with others. All the things you once believed to be true and real are up for change and transformation.

This is also a time when you may want to escape reality, but the only way to be free of it is to face it and stand up to it. When you face your reality, you gain the power and strength to create the reality of your dreams. Each of us has a responsibility to create the most beautiful life possible for ourselves. The Neptune Square transit often highlights that responsibility for us in a unique way.

Neptune moves slowly, taking 165 years to orbit the Sun. It also spends up to fourteen years in a particular zodiac sign. For this reason, the sign your Neptune is in at the time of your birth indicates your generational lessons. For more of a personal look, you will want to pay extra attention to the house placement.

♆♈ | NEPTUNE IN ARIES OR FIRST HOUSE

GENERATIONAL LESSON to become the hero of your own life

Neptune in Aries is the hero coming to save us from our troubles. This hero promises to take away all of our pain and suffering and to make things right again. Like all things Neptunian, the illusion eventually fades and we are left feeling manipulated and taken advantage of.

Neptune in Aries may paint the picture of needing a hero to swoop in and save us, but this is the illusion. In truth, the only person who can save us is ourselves. Sure, we can reach out to others for support and guidance, but no one else can step in and make the changes that are needed.

For many of us, the true hero we are waiting for lives within us. We have the power to make the changes and take the steps needed to create the life we desire. No one else knows what it's like to walk in our shoes; no one else knows what calls to our soul except ourselves. Stepping up to be the champion and hero of your own life is the message when Neptune is in Aries.

Neptune is in Aries from 2025 through 2039. During this time, we have to be mindful of giving our power away and making sure we are claiming it for ourselves. True power unfolds when we radically love and accept all of who we are, and then use that to find ways to be of service to ourselves and to those around us.

♆♉ | NEPTUNE IN TAURUS OR SECOND HOUSE

GENERATIONAL LESSON to find abundance by working in unity with nature and all of life

With Neptune in Taurus, it is important we connect to the Earth and remember it is a precious resource that must be loved and not abused. On one level, Neptune in Taurus can make us greedy and can lead to the abuse of natural resources. It can cause us to want to take and take, under the belief that we are building a better life. But once the Neptune veil has been removed, we can see that our ways of greed are not only unsustainable, but not as fulfilling as they promised to be.

With Neptune in Taurus, the call is to work in harmony with the cycles of the Earth. Rather than taking, we are asked to work with nature and tune in to the abundance it is offering us. When we learn to work with its rhythms, we find there is always enough and there is always plenty for all. Neptune in Taurus calls for us to balance the scales and create more equality, especially when it comes to the way the planet's resources are being used.

Neptune is in Taurus from 2038 through 2052. During this time, we may see changes to the way our planet's resources are being used. This may also bring a shift of wealth and power. Neptune in Taurus is also a time of increased chances of flooding and tsunamis.

♆♊ | NEPTUNE IN GEMINI OR THIRD HOUSE

GENERATIONAL LESSON to balance the mind and the soul,
and to have the two working in harmony

Neptune in Gemini is the wise old sage sitting atop the mountain. From down below, it looks like the sage knows it all. There are tales of how wise the sage is, and how they can offer solutions to all of life's problems. Upon taking the weeks-long and treacherous trek to the top of the mountain, you arrive to realize you didn't need to be there in the first place. Everything you learned by making that trek has taught you everything you need to know about what you were coming to ask. From the top of the mountain, your problems look so much smaller—but this has nothing to do with the sage and everything to do with your perspective.

As you took the trek to the top of the mountain, you had to wrestle with your body, mind, and soul. You had to allow all three to work as one; otherwise, you wouldn't have been able to make the journey. Your physical body had to work with your mind so you could break through the barriers of exhaustion and physical limits. Your soul had to feel the passion and desire, the yearning to get to the top. All three working together is often how we find the solutions to our problems and navigate through our lives. With Neptune in Gemini, we are called to take a mind, body, and soul approach to our lives. The Gemini twins want us to build that bridge between the heavens and the earth, and Neptune's presence simply amplifies that. By balancing our inner world, we find balance in our outer world.

Neptune will enter Gemini in 2052 through 2066, and there may be a greater push to acknowledge the connection between the mind, body, and soul.

♆♋ | NEPTUNE IN CANCER OR FOURTH HOUSE

GENERATIONAL LESSON to follow our hearts and build supportive family

Your heart has an incredibly powerful energy field, and when we give ourselves permission to use it, we can tap into a new power and abilities we never realized before. With Neptune in Cancer, our heart field energy is amplified and it is easier to tune in to its wisdom and potential. We may also feel more compassionate toward one another or more focused on creating loving and supportive communities and families.

While our heart carries its own wisdom, we cannot ignore the wisdom of our mind in the process. Sometimes our heart knows the way, but sometimes we also need the grounding and structure that comes from our rational and logical mind. Neptune in Cancer challenges us to balance these dynamics and learn when to follow our heart and when we need to ground ourselves. Neptune in Cancer can also stir the desire to create and honor family values. We may feel a push toward creating a more supportive family environment or, alternatively, working to create clearer and more balanced boundaries with our family.

Neptune will enter Cancer from 2065 to 2079. During this time, we may see shifts when it comes to understanding the energy field or "brain" of our heart, family dynamics, and how we choose to define family.

♆ ♌ | NEPTUNE IN LEO OR FIFTH HOUSE

GENERATIONAL LESSON to bring beauty to the world through art and entertainment

Neptune in Leo wants to be adored, loved, cherished, and praised. It has incredible artistic talents too. When it brings out its inner genius in a work of art, it longs to get the attention it deserves. Neptune in Leo is definitely a creative force we can all take and use in our lives. We also have to remember our creative efforts, and what we put into the world is not a measure of our value or worth. Neptune in Leo loves praise, but the best praise it can receive is the praise from itself.

Of course, it is always nice to receive praise, especially from those we love and care about. How many of us as children longed for our parents to say, "We are so proud of you," or longed for our crush at school to compliment us. When we are children, receiving attention, admiration, and praise can help us thrive. A baby cries not just because it needs something but because it also wants to know it's safe and that its needs will be met.

Receiving admiration and praise is a human need, but as we get older, we tend to fall into a trap when we look for or even chase external praise. When we want those around us to love and admire us, we tend to lose our way, and act not from a place of truth but from a place of trying to please. Over time, this throws us out of our natural alignment and takes us away from our true selves. True alignment and power come when we learn to praise and ultimately love ourselves. While we can search for love from others, we cannot appreciate it to its fullest until we have learned to wholeheartedly love ourselves. When you are taking your final breaths on this planet, the thing that matters is how you feel about yourself and not what others think of you. And in those final moments, you deserve to be loving yourself and the life you've led.

Neptune will enter Leo in 2080, and at this time, we are likely to see a shift when it comes to art and entertainment. Perhaps on a more subtle level, loving ourselves will become all the more important.

♆

♆ ♍ | NEPTUNE IN VIRGO OR SIXTH HOUSE

GENERATIONAL LESSON to find the sacred in the mundane

Neptune in Virgo can be summed up by the Zen quote: "Before enlightenment, chop wood, carry water. After enlightenment, chop wood, carry water." Finding enlightenment, which is what Neptune is here to help us do, is not about ascending to some magical, mystical land where we are free of our earthly duties. Rather, finding enlightenment is finding the bliss and peace while we are here, and while we are doing mundane tasks like chopping wood and carrying water. Neptune in Virgo wants us to find the sacred in all we do, in the routines we create, in the jobs we head off to each morning.

Neptune in Virgo wants us to find the spiritual in the everyday. How often have you found yourself doing a mundane task and drifting off into another world? Before you know it, all this time has passed and you wonder where you have been! During moments like this, without realizing it, you have entered a meditative state. Your mind may have been thinking, but part of you escaped from reality, got immersed in what you were doing, and lost track of time. Taking that sensation and applying it in a more mindful way is all meditation is. We can enter this state not just on a meditation cushion or in yoga class, but all throughout the day. Even the most banal tasks can become sacred when we allow them to be.

Navigating life on Earth is not about transcending it to some mythical state of being, it is being fully alive and fully present when doing all the things your human self requires you to do, such as eating, sleeping, and paying taxes! With Neptune in Virgo, we can be drawn to and reminded of this, and we may even reach new states of enlightenment when we embrace this mindset. Neptune will be in Virgo when we cross into the next century, and it will be interesting to see what new world that brings.

♆ ♎ | NEPTUNE IN LIBRA OR SEVENTH HOUSE

GENERATIONAL LESSON to reexamine justice and what is fair

What is fair and what is right? That is the realm Neptune in Libra covers. Libra is the sign of justice and fairness, but Neptune can cloud the waters. What is *really* fair? And is doing the fair thing always the right thing to do? With Neptune in Libra, the water can get muddy and our judgment can be clouded. This is only so we can stretch our minds and imaginations and reconsider what we deem as fair and what we deem as right, and when it's acceptable or not for these two ideas to cross over.

Neptune in Libra is also sensitive and creative. It can bring new fashion or design trends, and often those with Neptune in Libra have a style and elegance to them. Having style and elegance is not so much about what you are wearing but more how you choose to carry yourself. When you are beautiful on the inside, it shines through and makes you beautiful on the outside. With Neptune in Libra, we may find ourselves wrapped up in beauty and buying products that promise us we'll look a certain way, but as the veil is removed and the illusion shattered, we again come to realize that beauty is how we feel about ourselves, not because we look a certain way or use a certain set of products.

Neptune was last in Libra in the mid-1940s and won't return for another 165 years. At this time, we may see beauty and fashion trends shift and change, and there may also be some world events that challenge the justice system.

♆ ♏ | NEPTUNE IN SCORPIO OR EIGHTH HOUSE

GENERATIONAL LESSON to shift darkness into light

Neptune in Scorpio helped inspire the sexual revolution of the 1960s. It took a taboo subject like sex and brought it out of the shadows and into the light. Neptune in Scorpio was a time when things that had remained private or personal suddenly started being talked about more openly, helping to create a dialogue that was liberating. All the shame buried beneath the surface floated to the top for clearing and for transformation.

With Neptune in Scorpio, you may have a strong desire to understand your emotions and your subconscious mind. It's not enough for you to live on the surface; you long to dive deep and to keep peeling back the layers until you find whatever it is that you are looking for. You may be drawn to understand the psychology of your brain or feel a need to understand the root of your emotions.

Neptune in Scorpio is also a sensitive and psychic placement, and you may feel your intuition strongly in your gut. Listen and trust your intuition, and follow through on its wisdom. In the beginning, it's hard to discern your intuition, but if it's not hurting anyone, it is always best to follow through on those hunches even when you are not sure, for that is how you learn to use it.

Scorpio also rules over divination, so you may feel drawn to working in or exploring this field. If you have ever been curious, buy a deck of tarot cards or pull up the natal chart of your friend and give your friend a reading—you may as well take advantage of these natural abilities that have been given to you! Neptune will next be in Scorpio in the twenty-second century, and at this time, we may see another sexual revolution or perhaps new breakthroughs in psychology and mental health.

♆♐ | NEPTUNE IN SAGITTARIUS OR NINTH HOUSE

GENERATIONAL LESSON to open people's minds to radical new ideas

Neptune in Sagittarius is big and expansive, and it opens your heart and mind to new possibilities and new ways of thinking about things. Neptune in Sagittarius can cause us to question the information we have been taught and inspires us to go into the world to experience things for ourselves. With Neptune in Sagittarius, there is a desire to break free from the traditions of our past or our culture and to find a new and more modern way of doing things.

Neptune in Sagittarius favors learning by experience. You can read all the books in the world and research all you like, but sometimes the only way to learn and understand something is to jump right in and get your feet wet. As Sagittarius is a fire sign, there is a strong desire to take this ethereal, watery, flowy energy of Neptune and turn it into action.

Having Neptune in Sagittarius makes you spontaneous and a little adventurous, and it also gives you a fierce streak of independence. You are not afraid to share your opinions and to let others know what you are thinking and feeling. As Neptune can create some fogginess, you may at times find yourself out of touch with those around you or blinded as to how your words may make others feel. You need to work on keeping yourself grounded and finding ways to express yourself that are thoughtful but still allow you to stay true to yourself.

Neptune was last in Sagittarius from 1970 to 1984. During this time, there was a strong push toward equal rights and gay rights. Sagittarius energy guided people to think bigger and opened people's minds to new ideas. More people felt comfortable sharing their opinions and speaking out against traditional establishments that needed to change.

♆♑ | NEPTUNE IN CAPRICORN OR TENTH HOUSE

GENERATIONAL LESSON to turn dreams into tangible realities

Neptune in Capricorn is about finding your center among the flow. Your gifts and talents in this life rest in keeping your cool and staying grounded, even as life is ebbing and flowing around you. Your generation is here to remind us all that our center and our state of balance are not about what is happening around us but what is happening inside of us.

With Neptune in Capricorn, there is a strong desire to be the unmovable tree in the wind, but this is a rigid and somewhat stressful way to move through life. It is far more powerful to be the grounded and rooted tree and to let your branches sway in the wind. By swaying, you allow yourself to go with the flow, rather than against it.

Neptune in Capricorn is powerful for manifestation. The dreamy quality of Neptune allows our imagination to soar, while the practical Capricorn helps us put pen to paper to get things done. With Neptune in Capricorn, there is no dream too big and no ambition too great. Get your dreams and ideas onto paper, and write down what you would like to create and achieve. Go big with it, and allow your imagination to take hold. Then, look back over what you wrote and see if you can make a bullet list of actions you can take to turn your dream into a reality. If you can dream it, you can do it. With Neptune in Capricorn, you have the gift of taking your wildest dreams and building them into concrete plans. Step by step and little by little, you can build anything.

Neptune was last in Capricorn from 1984 through 1998. During this time, the first e-commerce stores came online. This must have sounded like a Neptunian dream to many, but with the help of practical and grounded Capricorn, these businesses are now a huge part of our everyday reality. It will be interesting to see what far-out dreams come into reality when Neptune next visits Capricorn.

♆ ♒ | NEPTUNE IN AQUARIUS OR ELEVENTH HOUSE

GENERATIONAL LESSON to inspire independent thinking and changes that benefit all

Neptune in Aquarius brings radical innovation and thinking outside of the box. There is also a strong push toward humanitarian efforts and bringing people together to build stronger and more sustainable communities.

The dreamy, ethereal energy of Neptune, mixed with the radical and forward-thinking Aquarius, gives you a sharp and inventive mind, one that is always coming up with new ideas and new inspirations. You may find it difficult to get your ideas onto paper or to bring them to life. To help with this, perhaps make a vision board or mood board to highlight the tone or feeling you are trying to convey.

Your ideas are supposed to be big and bold, so don't censor yourself just because those around you don't understand. You want to be open to feedback, but part of your purpose in this life is to switch things on their head and to think about things in a new and almost revolutionary way.

Along with having many bright ideas, you are also a humanitarian at heart. You may feel drawn to make a difference to the planet and to the lives of others. In fact, part of your purpose and passion in this life stems from helping and being of service to others. When you are feeling stressed or anxious, one of the best remedies for you is to put your own problems to the side for a moment and go help someone else. This simple act of being of service to others can instantly brighten your mood and can help you see your own troubles in a new light and a new perspective. When you reach out and help others, the help you offer can also teach you something about what you need to start doing yourself.

Neptune was last in Aquarius from 1998 through 2012, and won't return again for another 165 years.

♆♓ | NEPTUNE IN PISCES OR TWELFTH HOUSE

GENERATIONAL LESSON to let go of the ego and find spiritual connection

Neptune is home in the sign of Pisces, so we get its energy to the fullest potential. Neptune in Pisces is about dissolving the ego to make way for the spirit to shine through. When we become aware of our egocentric habits, like living from a scarcity mindset, feeling the need to compete with others, feeling superior or less than others, or being in a judgmental headspace, we are able to transcend them and shift past limited beliefs into something more loving and unifying.

It takes practice to ascend our ego, and at first it can be challenging. But the more we identify the ego mind when it arises, the easier it becomes to switch out of our ego and reach for the voice of our truth. After all, we are not our thoughts, we are the observer of our thoughts—so why not choose thoughts that lift us up and make us feel good, and why not choose to see others in the same light? This doesn't mean we give people a free pass and allow them to disrespect us, but we can move from a place of nonjudgment and recognize being mistreated by others seldom has anything to do with us, and is more to do with their state of mind.

Learning to create healthy boundaries is important with Neptune in Pisces. Because the energy can be so unconditional and loving, we want to make sure we are also taking the measures needed to protect ourselves. It is perfectly okay to love from a distance, and it is perfectly okay to love someone and not want them in your life. Neptune in Pisces has the power to teach us unconditional love, and the lesson is there if we wish to take it. The first step is breaking out of the ego and learning to love ourselves unconditionally first.

Neptune in Pisces is also highly creative and can bring advancements to creative industries, in particular to the music industry, seeing as Pisces rules over music.

Neptune is in Pisces from 2012 through 2026. During this time, more people wake up to realize there is so much more to life than what we can see and what we have been told. There is a greater interest in spirituality, and more people find comfort in things such as crystals, self-help work, and meditation. As Pisces is the last sign of the zodiac and the home of Neptune, it can also bring an ending and a new beginning on a global level. We may see one world fall away and a new one emerge once Neptune is ready to move on to Aries.

13

Pluto

ZODIAC RULER Scorpio
KEYWORDS death/rebirth, transformation, metamorphosis,
shadow work, power, underworld, obsession
RULES OVER power positions, great wealth, dictatorships,
abuse, secrets, higher consciousness, detoxing

Pluto is the planet of death and rebirth. Its energy governs the process of the phoenix rising from the ashes. At first, something needs to burn and die, and from these ashes, a rebirth is possible that allows us to tune in to a greater power than before. As Pluto moves so slowly, the sign it falls in is more generational than personal. The house placement will be more personal, as it indicates where you will express this energy.

PLUTO: LORD OF THE UNDERWORLD

Pluto is considered the Lord of the Underworld, and it is about digging through our shadows and the darker, deeper stuff to transform it into light. Pluto is a little dark and mysterious, and when its energy is highlighted in our chart or in the sky, it often signals we are about to go through a transformation.

Pluto was the first planet I studied when I started my journey with astrology. There was something about its ability to transform and shift things that captivated me. To this day, when I am reading someone's chart, one of the first things I look at is what Pluto is up to. Pluto's activity shows me where transformation may be occurring or where the person may be moving into a new state of being.

Like a caterpillar turning into a butterfly or a snake shedding its skin, Pluto's work is powerful and often hidden. We can't see the transformation taking place until it's completed, which is why Pluto's energy can often get missed. It tends to work in the underworld or in the subconscious, and it's not until it's finished that we can see the results and the change that has taken place.

Pluto moves the slowest of all the planets, taking 248 years to orbit the Sun. This makes Pluto's movements even more powerful as they are so long lasting. It also means that some people will experience Plutonian energy more than others.

Look to where Pluto is in the sky right now and then match its location in your chart. For example, if Pluto is currently at 1 degree of Aquarius, look to where 1 degree of Aquarius falls in your chart.

If Pluto is within a few degrees of your ascendant, descendant, nadir, or any of your natal planets, that area of your life will be under Pluto's spell of transformation.

If you do have Pluto crossing a sensitive point in your chart or aligning with your Sun or Moon, know that it is pretty special! It also indicates that your soul signed up for a big transformation in this life and wanted to move into a new and higher vibration.

Pluto's transformational work usually takes about a decade to complete because it moves so slowly, but sometimes it can bring obvious and clear shifts into our lives. When Pluto is around, something has to be burned away. There has to be some destruction of life as we once knew it in order to pave a new way.

Pluto's transformation can be painful and challenging. There is often a type of death involved that can lead to feelings of grief, confusion, and despair. Pluto can feel dark and a little depressing, and it can be hard to see the light at the end of the tunnel.

Like the caterpillar in the cocoon, it has to go through the darkness to move through the transformation. I often wonder if the caterpillar knows what is happening to it or if it feels it has entered some state of death and endless darkness. That is what Pluto's energy can feel like sometimes. But eventually, this passes. Once Pluto has completed its work, the chrysalis breaks and the butterfly is free. The life it once knew of crawling and nibbling on green leaves is over. It can now fly from flower bud to flower bud in a matter of seconds, and its body is a brilliant array of colors. Just like the metamorphosis of the caterpillar, we have to go through the darkness when Pluto is near. The darkness always leads the way to the light, and eventually we get to experience life with a new set of wings.

While none of us will ever get to experience a Pluto Return, we do get to experience a Pluto Square at the age of 36 to 39. This connects closely to the same timing as the Neptune Square and the Uranus Opposition, so all of them are working together and in unison to create a shift in our lives.

Pluto Square (age 36 to 39): Under your Pluto Square, you undergo an evolution that sees you grow into your power or awaken to a deeper level. The stirrings of your Pluto Square pave the way for your Neptune Square and your Uranus Opposition that also follows.

Under your Pluto Square, you may also push past some fears that you held in your younger years, and you realize you are far more powerful than these fears allowed you to believe. Sometimes the only way to transcend these fears is to face them. When you face fearful challenges, know that this is your opportunity to rise above it and face them head-on.

With Pluto, there is always the sense of something needing to be destroyed or some destruction taking place in order to birth something new. Nature can be a powerful teacher for us, as it too is constantly going through cycles of death and rebirth. In the autumn season, the leaves fall from the trees and decompose, nourishing the soil and the earth. The trees remain bare and naked, perhaps feeling a little exposed, but also in need of a rest. Then once spring emerges, tiny green buds appear and new leaves are formed and grow until the autumn returns again.

This constant cycle of life and death that we see in nature reminds us that just like the leaves, we have to learn how to let go and surrender to the ebbs and flows and changes that life brings. They are always temporary, and every state we find ourselves in will pass. When you are going through a difficult transformation or if you notice Pluto moving into a prominent place in your chart, allow nature to be your guide and recognize that just like the phoenix, you will rise from the ashes with bigger wings and a brighter inner fire.

♀♈ | PLUTO IN ARIES OR FIRST HOUSE

GENERATIONAL LESSON Who am I?

The Lord of the Underworld in the sign of the warrior helps us claim our power and remember that true power comes when we allow our independent spirit to shine. When we honor our unique spark and feel confident in who we are, there is no limit to what we can achieve or how far we can rise.

Pluto in Aries is fiery, passionate, and wants to keep transforming to discover new adventures and new limits of its potential. This can also be a destructive combination, as Pluto in Aries is not afraid to make things burn big and bright to bring about the change it is looking for. You are not afraid to explore things on a deeper level, and there is a good chance that your soul signed up for a life of transformation. You have a strong desire to keep peeling back the layers and revealing new dimensions and truths from inside of yourself.

Pluto in the first house can also indicate that you are destined to go through a transformative life experience that will bring lasting change.

♀♉ | PLUTO IN TAURUS OR SECOND HOUSE

GENERATIONAL LESSON What am I holding on to?

The Lord of the Underworld in the sign of the methodical and practical bull is not always the best fit. Pluto wants to transform, to set things alight, and watch them burn so something new can take its place. Taurus wants to control and take its time figuring out what needs to go and what needs to stay.

Pluto dominates here, so it is best to surrender to the flow and allow whatever needs to go to go, without feeling the need to hold on. The more we attach and try to grasp at things, the more stressed we become, and we are less likely to recognize the new opportunities when they arise. Sometimes we attach ourselves to things or ideas because we think they will make us feel better or because they give us a sense of identity. No "thing" or belief is really who we truly are.

Taurus wants us to hold on to things because it brings a sense of comfort and stability. Pluto reminds us that sometimes we have to be on unstable ground to transform and push ourselves to the next level. When you discover the truth of who you are and learn to stand in your power, it will be easier for you to trust the flow of what leaves and enters your life.

♀♊ | PLUTO IN GEMINI OR THIRD HOUSE

GENERATIONAL LESSON How do I express myself?

The Lord of the Underworld in the sign of the twins wants to transform the ways we choose to think about things and act on things. When Pluto is in Gemini, our mind undergoes a transformation, shifting and changing, so it can reach new levels of understanding, communication, and compassion.

With our mind transformed, we can get to work on taking new actions in our physical lives. Pluto in Gemini takes on two personas: one helps us change things from an internal level and the other helps us change things on an external level.

Very often, it's the internal shift that has to come first. As we change our perspective and learn to look at things differently, the things we are looking at tend to change.

You have the power when it comes to your voice and the messages you have to share with the world. When you speak, people tend to listen, so use your gifts of communication to get your ideas and thoughts into the world.

♇♋ | PLUTO IN CANCER OR FOURTH HOUSE

GENERATIONAL LESSON What does family mean to me?

The Lord of the Underworld in the sign of the crab allows us to feel our emotions deeply. Our sensitivity is heightened, and we are able to become more aware of our energetic body or our life force energy. Our psychic abilities or intuition can also be heightened with this placement.

With Pluto in Cancer, there is a strong instinct to protect and stand up for things that matter to you. You may feel a strong sense of allyship when it comes to your family, culture, or ancestry. Your family life is at the heart of any transformations you undertake. You need to be extra mindful of giving away your identity to family structures or rules, or to the wants and desires of the world around you. You may feel like you are losing yourself at times, but by standing up for yourself and going after the things you love and desire, you are able to claim more of your personal power.

♇♌ | PLUTO IN LEO OR FIFTH HOUSE

GENERATIONAL LESSON What is love?

The Lord of the Underworld in the sign of Leo the lion is an interesting combination. The lion is bright, bold, and sunny, whereas Pluto prefers the comfort of the shadows.

With Pluto in Leo, we may find ourselves continually having to transform and change our lives when we are led by our ego rather than our heart. Pluto in Leo can create a sense that all that glitters isn't gold. We may find ourselves swept up by someone or something we desire, only to find out it's not what was promised or that the rug was pulled out from under us at the last second. These lessons cannot be avoided sometimes, but this is when you are called to transform and make decisions from a place of heartfelt truth rather than your ego. The ego likes you to believe that you need more in order to be happy and satisfied. The heart knows that true happiness and satisfaction have nothing to do with your external reality and everything to do with your internal one.

Your relationships can be highly transformative and revealing for you. It is through your relationships, especially romantic ones, that you are able to discover more of who you are and what love means to you.

♀ ♍ | PLUTO IN VIRGO OR SIXTH HOUSE

GENERATIONAL LESSON What makes me worthy?

The Lord of the Underworld in the sign of the independent virgin is about taking back and claiming your personal power. It is about recognizing how strong you are and not letting your goals, dreams, and desires fall by the wayside to please or appease others.

With Pluto in Virgo, there may be some transformation to go through in regard to this. You may find that you have to give things up to discover your true independence again, or you may find that life removes things from your path so you can step into your full independence. Being independent is not about being alone or doing things on your own; it is about finding the strength and resilience you need to create the best and most fulfilling life for you, regardless of your circumstances.

Pluto in the sixth house especially can indicate a strong mind–body connection. When you are feeling something on a mental level, you tend to notice it showing up on a physical level, so it's important to keep your stress levels under control.

♀ ♎ | PLUTO IN LIBRA OR SEVENTH HOUSE

GENERATIONAL LESSON What do I stand for?

The Lord of the Underworld in the sign of the scales is about transforming things to create more balance. When the scales get tipped in one direction over the other, Pluto begins weaving its magic and reminding us of the importance of keeping things in balance. As part of this process, it may also tilt the scales in one direction to help us find our center.

Sometimes we have to be pushed to extremes to find our middle ground. Pluto in Libra is pushing boundaries and helping us find a new center. Just when we think we have it all figured out, we are challenged and pushed yet again to find a new truth. Life is a constant process of losing yourself only to find yourself again. Embrace the unknown and the uncertainty when it arises, and know that these are points in your life when you are doing the most growing.

Pluto in the seventh house can indicate a marriage or partnership that is deeply transformative.

♀ ♏ | PLUTO IN SCORPIO OR EIGHTH HOUSE

GENERATIONAL LESSON What does it mean to die?

Pluto is ruled by Scorpio, so the Lord of the Underworld feels most at home in the sign of the scorpion. The scorpion itself is a symbol for change and transformation. Like the snake, the scorpion sheds its skin about six times in its life so it can be reborn. When the scorpion sheds its skin, it is at its most vulnerable and the process can be stressful. After the scorpion has shed its skin, it's also very delicate for a few days as its shell becomes hard again. Just the same, when we go through our own metamorphosis, we, too, may feel vulnerable and stressed. We may wish to go into hiding and feel the need to hold ourselves back and make ourselves small. But eventually, our outer shell toughens once again.

With Pluto in Scorpio, transformation is the name of the game. You came into this life to keep shedding your skin and reinventing yourself as you move through your life journey. You are not likely to go through one significant metamorphosis, but several. You are always in the process of peeling back layers and looking to understand yourself on deeper levels. The surface level doesn't interest you; you crave deeper connections with yourself, others, and the world. Pluto in the eighth house can also indicate psychic and intuitive gifts.

♀ ♐ | PLUTO IN SAGITTARIUS OR NINTH HOUSE

GENERATIONAL LESSON What is freedom?

The Lord of the Underworld in the sign of the arrow of the archer is about transforming to find a greater freedom. This sense of freedom can come on a mental level through an expansion of ideas and beliefs, especially through higher education. It can also manifest on a physical level through traveling to far-off destinations or finding the freedom to go after your own dreams and goals. You seek a deeper meaning when it comes to life. You don't want to skim the surface; you want to dive in and understand things on all levels of your being.

THE MILLIONAIRE'S ASPECT

It's a rare combination, but having Pluto and Sagittarius's ruler, Jupiter, conjunct or within 5 to 7 degrees of each other in your natal chart is known as the millionaire's aspect and can indicate great wealth and prosperity.

With Pluto in Sagittarius, there are no boundaries or limits on what you can achieve in this life, and there is a sense that life is an adventure that is meant to be explored. You don't want to commit to one thing; you want to be able to taste and experience all of what life has to offer. Allowing yourself to explore helps take you to new levels of consciousness. Allowing your mind to expand to new dimensions helps you find a greater freedom and a deeper sense of truth of who you truly are.

♇♑ | PLUTO IN CAPRICORN OR TENTH HOUSE

GENERATIONAL LESSON What is true power?

The Lord of the Underworld in the sign of the sea goat is about transforming the rules and regulations we have chosen to live by. Sometimes these rules and regulations are carried down through generations and are never really questioned, but when Pluto is in Capricorn, their time is up for renewal and changes need to be made. The way things were done that could be seen as standard, traditional, and tried and true are all up for review so progress can be made.

Pluto in Capricorn indicates you like to shake up the status quo and get people to think differently about why they are choosing to do things. Understanding our motivation for doing things can help us live a life that is more aligned with the type of person we want to be, rather than who the world is telling us to be. Pluto in Capricorn is about taking responsibility for the changes we wish to see in our own lives, rather than waiting for others to make the changes for us.

Pluto in the tenth house can indicate great power and success when it comes to your career.

♇♒ | PLUTO IN AQUARIUS OR ELEVENTH HOUSE

GENERATIONAL LESSON How am I connected?

The Lord of the Underworld in the sign of the water bearer is about creating a new world—one that is guided by equality for the collective. With Pluto in Aquarius, there is a focus on finding ways to support the whole community rather than just the individual. There is a desire to transform the world through focusing on strengthening communities. When we work together, we become stronger and we are able to see with more clarity how best to support and lift up one another.

Pluto in Aquarius indicates transformation when it comes to the structure and framework of society. It indicates changes in how we come together to support ourselves and each other. Pluto in Aquarius can also bring changes to humanitarian efforts and how we approach the giving and spending of resources. The psychic energy of both Pluto and Aquarius also merge to bring deeply spiritual and profound experiences that can lead to healing.

Pluto in the eleventh house can indicate a karmic friendship or a platonic soul mate connection that you are destined to experience in this life.

♇♓ | PLUTO IN PISCES OR TWELFTH HOUSE

GENERATIONAL LESSON What is real and what is illusion?

The Lord of the Underworld in the sign of the two fish swimming in opposite directions is a magical and mystical placement. We are likely to see the uncovering of some deep, dark secrets that can lead to incredible revelations and transformations. There may be a shift to a more spiritual way of life and a deeper understanding of the power that can occur when we all take steps to raise our level of consciousness.

Pluto in Pisces can also bring advancements in how we understand consciousness and the way our mind works. There are opportunities here for deep and lasting transformation through the discoveries that are made, and perhaps we will never be able to think about ourselves or our existence in the same way again.

Pluto in the twelfth house can indicate skeletons that need to be unearthed from your closet, not just from this life but from previous lifetimes too. Even though this work can be tiring, it is well worth it. As you keep digging and facing your fears and confronting the things that keep you up at night, you are returning to a new power and a new strength. This is also a very psychic placement, indicating gifts of mediumship.

IS THERE A GODDESS OF THE UNDERWORLD?

Beyond Pluto is another dwarf planet called Eris. Eris is the Goddess of Strife and Discord whose energy is very similar to both Pluto and Mars. It is said to bring a sense of chaos, but this chaos only serves to lift us to a new challenge and a greater purpose. Just like Pluto brings a fire that burns things to ashes, Eris brings chaos and discord that eventually leads us to find a new path and a new way forward.

Bringing It All Together

Now that you have reached the end of the book, you should have a deeper understanding of some of the core themes of your life and your soul's journey in this incarnation. If it feels like a lot of information, don't worry. Just take what resonates with you at this point in your life and leave the rest. Who knows where your life journey will take you and how you may relate to things further down the road.

Astrology is an intuitive art form, so feel free to trust your intuition and allow it to guide you. While we have dissected the chart piece by piece, we also look at the chart in its totality. The best way to do this is through your intuition. As you trust yourself and the knowledge you have obtained from reading this book, you will find that you won't have to keep referring to which planet is where and what aspect it's making. Instead, you will find the planets speaking to you and drawing your attention through your intuitive feelings to the things you need to be aware of.

Using your intuition can help you narrow the focus of your birth chart and can help astrology become a little less technical and more creative.

All the planets in our cosmic skies tell a story. We can use these stories to help create deeper understanding in our lives and find where we can best use the energy that has been given to us.

While this book has set you up with the basics of astrology, there is still so much more to learn. Even for me, I am still learning new things and discovering new wisdom that the planets have to offer. I hope that by reading this book, you feel empowered and a little closer to the lessons, gifts, and messages of your soul.

ON WHICH PLANET SHOULD I FOCUS?

Now that you are at the end of the book, set everything you have learned aside for a moment. Try this quick exercise: Use your intuition to answer: "Which planet do I connect with the most?" The first answer that arises is the one you should go with. Whatever planet resonates the most for you right now is the planet that carries the messages you need the most.

Resources

Visit foreverconscious.com for the latest intuitive astrology updates, including monthly forecasts, moon rituals, and more.

HOW TO DRAW YOUR BIRTH CHART

There are so many free online tools that will draw up a free natal birth chart for you. Check out astro.com, astro-charts.com, or alabe.com for some good options.

HOW TO FIND THE CURRENT TROPICAL POSITIONS OF THE PLANETS

Locating the current position of the planets can be done using an Ephemeris. You can find them online or in book format. A popular book is *The New American Ephemeris*. You can also use any of the astrology software/apps listed below.

ASTROLOGY SOFTWARE/APPS

Time Passages and Solar Fire are great for birth charts, keeping track of the planets, and drawing more advanced charts.

Acknowledgments

In gratitude to all the astrologers who came before me—the ones whose blogs I read, whose books I borrowed from the library, and whose videos I watched on this journey of learning the art and magic of the stars. Thank you to Jill Alexander and the team at Quarto and Fair Winds Press, the wonderful editor, Jenna Nelson Patton, and literary agent, Giles Anderson. And finally, a big, heartfelt thank you to all the readers of foreverconscious.com: Your enthusiasm to keep learning and your words of encouragement have guided me further on my journey of decoding the stars. This book would not be possible without all of you.

About the Author

Tanaaz Chubb is an intuitive writer and creator of foreverconscious.com—one of the largest astrology and spiritual blogs on the Internet. From a young age, Tanaaz felt very connected to the spirit world, and much of her writing comes from her connection with the Divine. She has written the books *The Power of Positive Energy, Messages for the Soul*, and *My Pocket Mantras*. Tanaaz hopes that her writings will empower, uplift, and inspire readers from all over the world. She was born and raised in Melbourne, Australia, but now lives in Los Angeles with her husband and Maltipoo. You can follow her on all major social media platforms under @ForeverConscious.

Index